"Steven W. Smith calls for preachers ... he calls a generation to cross-centered preaching in which the preacher surrenders everything to the high calling and the urgent purpose of preaching the cross of the Lord Jesus Christ. Smith's example is the apostle Paul and his goal is to see a generation of preachers follow the example of the great apostle. In *Dying to Preach*, Smith offers compelling biblical insights and keen proposals that will transform preaching and produce preachers who will preach the cross and nothing less. This is a timely book and a much needed contribution."

—R. ALBERT MOHLER JR.
President, The Southern Baptist Theological Seminary

"While most Christian preachers would assume that preaching is about the atonement of Christ, few would have the ability to ask what that means for the preacher and the pulpit. In the introduction, Steven W. Smith gives the fundamental premise of the book when he asks in effect, 'Who owns the pulpit?' This unique and remarkable book examines both the impact and the message of the cross on Christian preaching. Anyone serious about pleasing God in the pulpit should make this volume a part of his library and his heart."

—PAIGE PATTERSON
President, Southwestern Baptist Theological Seminary

"What you say is more important than how you say it. But how you say it is important! Steven W. Smith gets this exactly right in a book that will instruct as well as inspire. Read it and be challenged. Read it and be blessed."

—DANIEL L. AKIN
President, Southeastern Baptist Theological Seminary

"This book reveals the attitude of preaching without ignoring the action, revisits the motive for preaching without neglecting its method, and reexamines the substance of preaching without discarding the importance of style. I highly commend this work for those who desire the power for preaching and want to preach with power."

—ROBERT SMITH JR.
Professor of Preaching, Beeson Divinity School of Samford University

"Steven W. Smith cogently argues the case that Paul's understanding of the ministry was dying so that others might live. Smith then applies this to the preaching act and brilliantly shows that the greatest metaphor for preaching the gospel is the gospel itself. Tragically, much of today's preaching eclipses the gospel. Smith issues a clarion call to a generation of preachers who will die to preach. This book reminds all of us who preach that we must die to our desires to entertain, to be cute and funny, and to tell story after story, in order that the true gospel might live. Buy it and read it once every year for the rest of your ministry."

—DAVID L. ALLEN
Dean, School of Theology, Southwestern Baptist Theological Seminary

"Jesus said, 'whoever wishes to save his life will lose it, but whoever loses his life for My sake and the gospel's will save it.' Steven W. Smith has taught us exactly how to lose our life in the pulpit. The church needs more crucified pastors in the pulpit, and *Dying to Preach* has shown us the way!"

—Greg Heisler
Assistant Professor of Preaching, Southeastern Seminary

"*Dying to Preach* is not another 'how-to' book that tries to change our practice of preaching through mechanics and newfangled methods. It's a fresh stab at changing the way we think about preaching, which ultimately will change how we do it. And that change takes us right back to the cross of Christ."

—Jim Shaddix
Senior Pastor, Riverside Baptist Church, Denver, Colorado

"Steven W. Smith, a dynamic communicator and a thoughtful scholar, shows us what it means to preach with power, authority, gravity, and fidelity. Read this book with a Bible in one hand and a blank page on your desk. It will make you want to get started on next Sunday's sermon!"

—Russell D. Moore
Dean, The Southern Baptist Theological Seminary

"Steven W. Smith is one of our shining lights in the field of sermon preparation. His training, experience as a preaching pastor, and fresh insights have uniquely qualified him to write this most helpful volume. Rather than dealing just with the mechanics of how to put together a sermon, Smith deals with the preacher dying to self so that the Christ of the cross may convey the glorious message of the gospel through a yielded spokesman. Read this book, incarnate its message, and you will become a preacher 'dying to preach.'"

—Jerry Vines
Pastor Emeritus, First Baptist Church, Jacksonville, Florida

"Steven W. Smith presents a Christ-centered, self-sacrificing understanding of the preaching task that calls the preacher to the suffering of the cross. This book brings to mind the challenge of Dietrich Bonhoeffer: 'When Christ calls a man, he bids him come and die.' Smith challenges us at the core of our personal identity by suggesting that 'the greatest threat to the pulpit is the giftedness of its preachers.'"

—Wayne V. McDill
Senior Professor of Preaching, Southeastern Seminary

"John the Baptist knew that he must decrease for Christ to increase. Steven W. Smith shares passionately how the preacher today will see little life in the pews until he sees much death in the pulpit."

—Johnny Hunt
Senior Pastor, First Baptist Church, Woodstock, Georgia

DYING
to Preach

Embracing the CROSS in the PULPIT

STEVEN W. SMITH

Kregel
Academic & Professional

Dying to Preach: Embracing the Cross in the Pulpit

© 2009 by Steven W. Smith

Published by Kregel Publications, a division of Kregel, Inc., 2450 Oak Industrial Dr. NE, Grand Rapids, MI 49505.

ISBN 978-0-8254-3897-4

Printed in the United States of America

3 4 5 6 7 8 / 21 20 19 18 17 16 15 14

For a generation dying to preach

Contents in Brief

Contents

Preface

If the cross is God's chosen means of salvation, why is it not also our means of communication? If God saved through the cross, can we not preach through the cross? If the cross was God's means, why is it not ours? Is God so crippled that He had to use the cross for salvation, and we so strong that we do not need the cross for our proclamation? If God will save through the abject humility of crucifixion, will He sanctify with messages from preachers who don't imitate the abject humility of crucifixion? Must not a message of death to life be communicated from a preacher who dies so that others might live? For the preaching act, this is the question: Can the message of the cross be mediated by a means other than a cross?

This short volume attempts to answer this question with one simple affirmation: The principal metaphor for the act of preaching the gospel is the gospel. The gospel is much more than preaching, but it is not less. Thus a cross *from* the pulpit logically means a cross *in* the pulpit. So every preacher dying to preach must die to preach.

A WORD ABOUT THE APPROACH

It is hard to read the New Testament and not come to the conclusion that spiritual vitality in God's people demands the death of many things in those who propagate the gospel. Christian ministry is the imitation of the gospel of Jesus Christ. More specifically, Christian ministry is dying so others might live.

However, communicating that reality is challenging. Our approach begins with Paul's ministry to the Corinthians. We begin here because in his ministry to the Corinthians, Paul was forced to defend himself, his character, motivations, and actions; in this defense, Paul provides the prototype for Christian ministry.

For this reason Paul's letters to the Corinthians yield the most abundant source material for understanding the relationship between the cross and the pulpit. Thus, the first chapter simply attempts to establish that Paul understood ministry as giving up his life so that others could live spiritually. The second chapter attempts to extend this thought on ministry in general to preaching in particular in 1 and 2 Corinthians. Admittedly, this can be slippery. It's not that the reality of a crucified pulpit is not there; however, Paul often is using words translated "preaching" when the context indicates he is talking about his ministry generally, rather than the act of proclamation specifically. So it would be exegetically dishonest, for example, to say, "Paul said in 2 Corinthians 4:5 that he does not preach himself, and he is meaning to say 'don't talk about yourself in the pulpit.'" Paul is defending the fact that he does not use ministry to advance personal agendas. However, if this is true of ministry in general, then it is *at least* true of preaching in particular. So in this way it seems fair to apply what Paul says of ministry in broader contexts to the act of preaching.

It is interesting that when Paul does describe his ministry in general, he describes it as a ministry of proclamation. He uses the word κηρύσσομεν, the herald. However, this is a book about preaching, and the concepts apply as they would in a book on other facets of ministry. So, just in case it is not clear later, please know that I am trying to establish what Paul meant generally about ministry and then suggest that what is true about ministry generally applies to preaching specifically, even if this disclaimer is not posted on subsequent pages.

Part 2 examines three other critical texts representative of this idea. There is certainly more in the New Testament about the idea of a cruciform life, but it would be impossible to suggest that we had broached the subject without, at the least, a closer look at 2 Corinthians 4:1–6; Colossians 1:24; and Hebrews 13:15. The treatment of these texts at times seems to bog down and at other times seems superficial. My desire is to make the application quickly in order to get to the point of all of this, which is the final section. Part 3 applies these truths to specific areas of preaching.

There is much more to say about this topic than has been said here. I have chosen brevity because, again, I want to get to the application and because much of what needs to be said about these texts already has been said very well in other volumes.

Perhaps more time should be spent on "classic" biblical texts on preaching. However, many of those texts, such as 1 Corinthians 2:1–5 and 2 Timothy 3 and 4, already have received good treatment. My purpose simply is to ask what it is about God's communication of Himself that should influence my communication of Him. And, naturally, texts that speak to God's communication of Himself are not necessarily about preaching. This is why I chose the word "Implications" in the title of part 2.

A Word About the Audience

As I look at a classroom full of students, my gut feels sick. The thrill of teaching preaching gives way to this obese stewardship. They have a small opportunity to think about preaching, and this is it. God help them to get it right. God help me to help them get it right. God help me to be clear.

This book took about five years to write and only a few days to pen. And whatever is to blame for the delay, the yield was that through interaction with students and the thrilling challenge of trying to communicate the practice of preaching, my understanding of preaching has radically changed in the same direction. I owe them an inestimable debt. It is toward them that this work is written; whoever might read it should understand the intended audience. So if students or pastors were to ask me why they should build their ministry around the explanation of texts of Scripture, this book would be my answer.

Acknowledgments

Each time I read an acknowledgments section in the front of a book, I wince. I feel like a personal thank-you is taking place publicly and, for the sake of those reading, this would be done better in private.

However, it is clear that only a spiritual plagiarist would take personal credit for what others have done—the only assumption one could make unless the author stops to set the record straight. So, in the spirit of setting things straight, I am indebted principally to my family. My parents, Bailey and Sandy Smith, and Ashley's parents, Ron and Kay Cherry, have been a deep encouragement in the process. Their lives and generosity are overwhelming.

There are many encouraging friends to thank, but I will do this personally as I would not know where to start or stop. I do need to thank Paige Patterson, who first encouraged me to study François Fénelon's *Dialogues on Eloquence*, a work whose influence is seen in part 3. Thanks to those who read drafts and offered much needed critique: Jason Duesing, Malcolm Yarnell, Pete Schemm, Calvin Pearson, Quincy Jones, and Todd Von Helms, and many students who read versions of the work and offered help. I thank Michael Graves for his exemplary scholarship and encouragement. Special appreciation to Jim Weaver for considering this project and encouraging its success. There are many others to thank, but special thanks should go to the Salem Baptist Church of Richmond, Virginia, for allowing me to work this out on a weekly basis for eight years; and to the Hillcrest Baptist Church of Cedar Hill, Texas, for allowing me to work this out while teaching it. Finally, I owe the deepest gratitude to my Ashley, who believed. I'm still shocked really—and overwhelmed. Thank you, love.

Surrendered Communication

There comes a time in the life of every preacher when he must decide who owns the pulpit. If the pulpit belongs to the people, then their desires will drive its content and presentation. If the pulpit belongs to the preacher, then his thoughts, intents, and desires will drive its content and presentation. If the pulpit is driven by delivery— eloquence, relevance, being trendy or intellectual—then it is driven by what style appears the best.

The contention of this book is that biblical preaching is driven by a higher desire than any of the things above. The preacher who is biblical has given up his preaching. He no longer owns it. Frankly, he has surrendered to the idea that preaching should be driven by any one of these factors.

The "drive" of preaching is birthed from the recognition that in order for Godlike results to take place, preaching must be surrendered to God, and the preacher must give his life in that surrender. In the same way that Adam was to take dominion over a creation that was not his, the preacher is to articulate a message that belongs to God. He is to have dominion over a task he will never own, for it was not his to begin with. Adam named, took dominion over, and possessed a creation he did not own but of which he was a steward.

In the same way, we put names to theological truths, build hermeneutical bridges, and apply eternal truths that belong to God alone. In other words, as the preacher grows more proficient in his task, less of him will be visible. So the Word of God increases in relationship to a willful decreasing of the preacher. We choose either to make much of God or to make much of the preacher. However, self-exaltation and God-exaltation cannot ride in tandem toward the goal of congregational maturity. To choose to let the Word of God live is also to choose to die to many other things. This work is offered to help those of us called out to live on death row.

This exchange, this dying to self so that the Word of God might live, I am tempted to call "vicarious" suffering since in a sense we are suffering on behalf of others. However, the concept of vicarious suffering is more precisely associated with Christ's work on the cross and therefore is not the best choice for describing the preacher's work.

Paul did not suffer on the Corinthians' behalf to intercept the wrath of God and therefore become their propitiation. Neither Paul's suffering for the Corinthians nor our suffering for those to whom we minister is vicarious in this way. Such suffering is vicarious only in the limited sense that an exchange takes place. Paul extended the sufferings of Christ to the Colossians (Col. 1:24); he died so that the Corinthians might live (2 Cor. 4:12). He was not offering a substitutionary atonement by bearing God's wrath; he was simply choosing to suffer in his body so that they might have spiritual life.

In this limited way, the sufferings of Christ are extended *vicariously* to those to whom Paul ministered. Similarly, an exchange takes place when a preacher chooses to suffer long hours in the study and potential misunderstanding by people and other pastors, all for the sake of others' spiritual health. This is a daunting challenge. It is a surrender that, as the apostle Paul would say in 2 Corinthians 4:12, "works [death] in us, but life in you."

The inestimable challenge of preaching is at once to grow in the development of the task while simultaneously giving it away, that is, being willing to die for people so that they might live. This means a preacher will care deeply about preaching while at the same time surrendering his communication to God. In this surrender, he is not only losing; he is also gaining. He is dying, and his people are living. The death to self that is demanded of the preacher works life in his people. In this way, the preacher becomes like Christ, who died so that we might live. If we do not die, they do not live. The exchange is real. The pulpit is to present a translucent soul laid over the vicarious suffering of our Lord, modeling His sacrifice. God help us to embrace the cross in the pulpit.

Part 1

The Cross in the Pulpit in Paul's Ministry

This section seeks to establish Paul's principal understanding of ministry to the Corinthians as dying for others. Further, the question of this death-to-life genre will be applied to the preaching act in Paul's ministry to the Corinthians.

[1]

Dying So Others Might Live (Part 1)

Paul's Ministry in Corinth

THE FRUSTRATION OF PREACHING

When Paul first walked the streets of Corinth, little could he have imagined how tough his ministry there would become. His heart would be broken, torn to shreds. His aspirations for the church at Corinth would be devastated. His dreams for them would never be realized. In fact, Paul would expend himself in public preaching, private conversation, and personal correspondence to encourage the sanctification of a group of people so stained by their surroundings they were hardly distinguishable from them. One man was sleeping with his stepmother (1 Cor. 5:1–2), people were drunk at the Lord's Supper (1 Cor. 11:17–22), and church members were suing each other (1 Cor. 6:1–6). As a whole they had no regard for one another's faith (1 Cor. 10:23). And this was the church crowd!

In some twisted way, it is encouraging for us preachers to realize that even Paul faced difficulty. Imagine a church culture so bent on perversion and hedonism that even the weight of Paul's apostolic ministry was not powerful enough to penetrate it. Listen to the frustration of the apostle when he writes,

For though I caused you sorrow by my letter, I do not regret
it . . . for I see that that letter caused you sorrow, though only
for a while. (2 Cor. 7:8)

Who is weak without my being weak? Who is led into sin
without my intense concern? (2 Cor. 11:29)

But I am afraid that, as the serpent deceived Eve by his craftiness, your minds will be led astray from the simplicity and
purity of devotion to Christ. (2 Cor. 11:3)

Every pastor can identify with Paul's pain. Preach to the people;
they do nothing. Love the people—nothing. Work for the people—
nothing. Perhaps this frustration is most clearly seen in the pulpit
ministry. We lay out our guts in the pulpit, and in response see stone-
cold faces with no ambition toward godliness or motivation to change.
We see only deeply embedded spiritual stubbornness and heartbreaking, disappointing, spiritual pride. Nothing is more discouraging to
a pastor than to give his life for fallen sheep, only to find that they
are perfectly content in their fallen state. Lethargy, complacency, and
mediocrity become the norm. Yet, this *is* pastoral ministry, and that
means finding the stamina to tread water while you explain to the
drowning that they are indeed drowning.

The tension between the unruly people and the frustrated preacher
often leads to a silent treaty. The treaty is not written anywhere. It
is not codified on paper as a bullet point in the bylaws, but it is real.

The treaty in essence states that if the pastor will leave the people
alone, they will leave him alone. Love, cherish, and nurture the flock,
and in Pastor Appreciation Month, you will get a greeting card af-
firming that the treaty is being honored. Often the treaty is affirmed
with conversations chock-full of church talk—*love you, appreciate you,
you are a blessing*—the translation of which is, "You are doing a really good job of not dealing with our sin publicly. Keep up the good
work, and we will not give you any trouble." At Christmas or on an

anniversary, the deacons affirm the treaty by honoring the mutual "Do Not Disturb" signs. The mutual neglect works beautifully.

I am not being cynical here about pastoral affirmation. Encouragement is desperately needed. Frankly, I am reflecting on my own experience of the temptation to live for the approval of people and not define my ministry by the pleasure of God.

However, it's possible that if you are reading this book, you are not comfortable with this vortex of apathy. You don't like the cowardly resignation to mutual mediocrity. It gets at you when you see people drowning in the wake of their own carnality. Although it seems impossible, you think that there has to be a way to jolt them out of the embrace of the commonplace and move them to spiritual vitality. Perhaps you thought at some point that this could be done from the pulpit. However you found that the harder you preach, the stronger is the resistance. Passionate pleas seem more like the ramblings of a frustrated prophet.

So how did Paul do it? How did he effect change in one of the most wicked, apathetic churches in history? The answer is simple and devastating: *Paul exchanged his life for the life of the Corinthians.* He died for them. He died so they could live. He suffered so they would not have to. He gave his life so they could have a life. He forced himself to a point of sickness so they could be well.

It seems the success of Paul's ministry was directly related to the amount he was willing to suffer. Or to say it another way, there is a definitive relationship between the suffering that Paul experienced and the spiritual vibrancy of the church. The more he suffered, the more they prospered. The more he died, the stronger they lived. The more he struggled, the more they were freed. The more he was deaf to the cries of his own flesh, the more they could hear the life-giving words.

Living for Others

On some level we all understand living for someone else.

I have never been to Green Bay, Wisconsin. It seems very cold. However, on December 23, 2003, I did something odd. I set aside time with my family to watch the Green Bay Packers play a football game. We set our dinner schedule before the game and later all huddled around the TV. Even my mother, who never understood or cared for the game, sat right beside us to watch.

The reason we were so interested was because the quarterback for Green Bay, Brett Favre, had lost his father in a tragic car accident the day before the game. Favre had a decision to make. This late in the season his absence could cause his team to forfeit any playoff hopes. Yet, how could he play in his emotional state? He played. He played like he had never played before. He set a personal best of four touchdowns and 311 yards passing in the first half alone.[1] The commentators kept referring to this remarkable feat. We kept throwing popcorn in the air. My mother wept.

This was all very odd. My emotions were on overload, even though I did not complete one pass, I did not lose my father, and I did not have an incredible game. What had happened was that I, with millions of others, entered vicariously into the pain and joy of Favre. The emotional rush was a vicarious identification with the athlete.

In case you think this is limited to testosterone-laden sporting events, this is exactly what happens when we watch an emotionally charged movie or read a touching novel. If I were to walk into the bedroom and see my wife crying while reading a novel, I might be tempted to say, "Sweetheart, you know that is not real. There really was not a triple amputee war veteran who came home to find his wife was in love with the Cuban pool boy!" To which she might reply, "Well, if that were you, how would you feel?"

This is it precisely. I am not a veteran, and I am not a quarterback. But if I were, how would I feel? This is what it means to live for others. I enter into someone's world, asking, if that were me, how would I feel? How should I feel? We all understand vicarious suffering on some level.

1. Pete Dougherty, "Dec. 22, 2003: Packers 41, Raiders 7," *Green Bay Press Gazette*, http://www.greenbaypressgazette.com/ic/favre/articles/favre_24223026.shtml (accessed July 29, 2008).

Suffering for Others

So here's a question: When I preach, how much am I willing to die so that others may be saved? Preaching is not a display case for rhetorical ability; it is not a place to show how traditional or trendy we are; it is not a place to fulfill aspirations of glory. The pulpit is a place to die so that others might live.

In order to develop this idea, the rest of this chapter will briefly attempt to establish that suffering for others was Paul's primary understanding of gospel ministry. Chapter 2 will then apply this to preaching by looking at Paul's specific application of this idea of suffering for others to the pulpit. Perhaps God will not call us to suffer like Paul. He was uniquely appointed as an apostle and therefore had to suffer in profound ways. However, the suffering we will have to endure is more real for the very reason that it is more pressing, more present. It is right here and now in our lives.

Before we scoot along in our little academic exercise, let me say that I believe this is a critical issue facing the church. It is nothing for us preachers to huddle in the halls of conferences and bemoan the lethargic state of the church. It is altogether something else for a man to boldly take his Bible and walk through texts with his people, giving the sense of it, and giving the implications of the text to people's lives.

This is a challenge so rich with difficulty that we hardly want to mount it. My father is wont to say that every major problem facing the church can be laid at the feet of a compromising pulpit. The social ills of our country, the immorality in our churches, and the soft pabulum being peddled as preaching would all be curbed if we would simply stay faithful to texts of Scripture.

I am intentionally not advocating a certain style of preaching. Explaining a text can take many different forms. In every context, in every style of preaching, in every place, the spiritual temperature of the church calls for men willing to die to their rights so that the Word of God may live in people. This is proclamation.

SUFFERING AS A MODEL OF MINISTRY IN 1 AND 2 CORINTHIANS

So this is it. Paul died so the Corinthians might live. No less than twenty times in his two extant letters to Corinth, he alludes to this idea of suffering for others. The references are so many that it's clear this is not a passing shot for Paul; this is his complete understanding of ministry.[2] There are so many texts that examining all of them would be a daunting task beyond the ambition of this chapter.

Here I only want to demonstrate that living and suffering was the principal metaphor by which Paul understood his ministry. To do this we will simply give an overview of these texts in chart form and then look at 1 Corinthians 9 as an example text where Paul explains clearly that he is suffering for the gospel so that others may be liberated by the gospel. In the following chapter, we will deal precisely with the question of preaching. For now, look at tables 1 and 2. It is fascinating how many times Paul directly identifies himself as one who dies so that his readers might live.

Table 1. Suffering of Paul for Others in 1 Corinthians

Text	Verse	Context
1 Cor. 2:2	*For I determined to know nothing among you except Jesus Christ, and Him crucified.*	Although highly educated, Paul limits his attention to the simple message of the gospel. Here he dies to the idea of parading his intellect because the clarity of the gospel is at stake. He wants them to know Christ more than knowing how much he knows.

---

2. There are several other texts in the New Testament that allude to this. However, since we are using Paul's ministry to the Corinthians as an example, texts will be limited in this chapter to 1 and 2 Corinthians. For examples of other important texts that include the idea of Paul's suffering for the people to whom he is ministering, see Colossians 1:24 and 1 Thessalonians 2:8.

Text	Verse	Context
1 Cor. 3:5	*What then is Apollos? And what is Paul? Servants through whom you believed, even as the Lord gave opportunity to each one.*	Here is the leading apostle of the church, the framer of Christian theology and missiology, identifying himself as nothing more than a slave. Paul's self-perception is that he is simply the conduit, the means, by which their belief came.
1 Cor. 4:9	*For, I think, God has exhibited us apostles last of all, as men condemned to death; because we have become a spectacle to the world, both to angels and to men.*	Here Paul refers to himself as "last of all" and a "spectacle." Roman gladiators would be paraded into the arena to die until the last group—the grand finale. Perhaps this is the apostle's reference.* This condemnation is both imposed by God and a self-condemnation. The idea is that as an apostle he is condemned to death by God. Also, the apostle condemns himself to death so that the Corinthians can be distinguished and have honor (v. 10). This is a perfect picture of suffering for others.
1 Cor. 4:10	*We are fools for Christ's sake, but you are prudent in Christ; we are weak, but you are strong; you are distinguished, but we are without honor.*	There are key contrasts in this verse: the apostles are fools, weak and dishonorable; the Corinthians are wise, strong and honored. The suffering the apostles endure (vv. 11–13) is a continuation of the idea of being a spectacle in v. 9. They are being paraded in humiliation for the spiritual well-being of the Corinthians.

---

* David Garland, *1 Corinthians*, Baker Exegetical Commentary on the New Testament (Grand Rapids: Baker, 2003), 140.

Text	Verse	Context
1 Cor. 8:12–13	*And so, by sinning against the brethren and wounding their conscience when it is weak, you sin against Christ. Therefore, if food causes my brother to stumble, I will never eat meat again, so that I will not cause my brother to stumble.*	The context of this passage refers to the practice of eating meat sacrificed to idols. Some Corinthians felt the freedom to do so, while others felt forbidden by their conscience. When we cause a brother to stumble (in this context by eating meat sacrificed to idols), we sin against Christ. This is because we are all a part of His body. To avoid this, Paul's drastic position is to clearly limit his personal freedom to protect any brother from stumbling. He will never eat suspect meat again. Again, this is a personal and willful choice to limit personal freedom to advance another's spiritual well-being.
1 Cor. 9:12	*If others share the right over you, do we not more? Nevertheless, we did not use this right, but we endure all things so that we will cause no hindrance to the gospel of Christ.*	The context of 1 Corinthians 9 is a discussion of the Corinthians' financial support of Paul specifically, and of ministers in general. His point is that while it is perfectly acceptable to receive financial assistance from them, Paul chooses not to do so in order not to become an impediment to the gospel.
1 Cor. 9:18	*What then is my reward? That, when I preach the gospel, I may offer the gospel without charge.*	Again, Paul is not willing to take that which is rightfully his. He works with his hands so that he might have the freedom to preach the gospel without charge.

Text	Verse	Context
1 Cor. 9:22	*To the weak I became weak, that I might win the weak; I have become all things to all men, so that I may by all means save some.*	The apostle is not afraid to "lower" himself to anyone's position. This acquiescence to the needs of others is for the express purpose of reaching them with the gospel.
1 Cor. 9:23	*I do all things for the sake of the gospel, so that I may become a fellow partaker of it.*	Paul connects his willingness to suffer so that some might be saved with his own participation in the gospel.
1 Cor. 9:27	*But I discipline my body and make it my slave, so that, after I have preached to others, I myself will not be disqualified.*	The apostle uses an athletic metaphor to describe how he competes to win. Part of the "beating of the body," the self-subjugation to suffering, is the willingness to suffer on behalf of others. Shockingly, he ties this to his own salvation, suggesting that if he were to leave the faith, he would illustrate that he was disqualified.
1 Cor. 10:33	*Just as I also please all men in all things, not seeking my own profit but the profit of the many, so that they may be saved.*	The conversation returns to the discussion of chapter 8 regarding eating and drinking. In 10:23 Paul affirms that all things should be done with others in mind. In 10:33 he encourages the Corinthians by his own example of doing all things so that others might be saved.

Table 2. Suffering of Paul for Others in 2 Corinthians

Text	Verse	Context
2 Cor. 1:5–6a	*For just as the sufferings of Christ are ours in abundance, so also our comfort is abundant through Christ. But if we are afflicted, it is for your comfort and salvation.*	The suffering of Christ is connected to the suffering that Paul endured for the advance of the gospel for the Corinthians. To put a fine point on it, he uses the afflicted/comforted tension to express his suffering for them. So this suffering for the gospel is suffering *in* Christ and *for* others.
2 Cor. 4:5	*For we do not preach ourselves but Christ Jesus as Lord, and ourselves as your bond-servants for Jesus' sake.*	Paul is explaining why he does not "preach himself." In vv. 3–4, Paul explains that the unbeliever is completely in the dark. Only Christ can remove the veil. The implication is that if he does not die to himself, if he does not surrender his rights, if he does not die so that others may live, others will stay in the dark. He is nothing more than a slave for Christ.
2 Cor. 4:10	*Always carrying about in the body the dying of Jesus, so that the life of Jesus also may be manifested in our body.*	Paul is always carrying about in his body the "dying of Jesus." He implies that Christ's vicarious suffering for them is imitated and extended by him.
2 Cor. 4:11	*For we who are constantly being delivered over to death for Jesus' sake, so that the life of Jesus may be manifested in our mortal flesh.*	Again, this suffering is an extension of Christ's suffering for them.

Text	Verse	Context
2 Cor. 4:12	*So death works in us, but life in you.*	This is perhaps the most precise statement on suffering for others. To effect the salvation of the people, death must be wrought in the preacher.
2 Cor. 5:13	*For if we are beside ourselves it is for God; if we are of sound mind, it is for you.*	Perhaps Paul is responding to the criticism that he was out of his mind. "Beside ourselves" implies insanity. So if he is insane, it is in his doctrinal commitments; it is in fidelity to God. Yet his true spiritual sanity affects their spiritual health.
2 Cor. 11:17	*Did I commit a sin in humbling myself so that you might be exalted, because I preached the gospel of God to you without charge?*	Paul is asking rhetorically if he did something wrong by sacrificing a love offering that he deserved so that he could preach the gospel without any cost to them. The obvious answer is no, again affirming his willingness to suffer for them.
2 Cor. 11:29	*Who is weak without my being weak? Who is led into sin without my intense concern?*	Paul is expressing precisely the idea of suffering for others. No one can suffer in the Corinthian church without Paul entering into his or her suffering.
2 Cor. 12:15	*I will most gladly spend and be expended for your souls.*	The context is the apostle's willingness to preach the gospel without charge. He is perfectly willing to come to them without any financial assistance, to expend himself, literally to spend freely.* So instead of charging for the gospel, Paul spends himself for the gospel.

---

* William Arndt and Wilbur Gringrich, *A Greek-English Lexicon of the New Testament* (Chicago: University of Chicago Press, 1958), 171.

Suffering on behalf of others is not one way among many to approach ministry. It is ministry. There is no life breathed into people without the death of the minister. The sweet smell of sanctification is preceded by the putrid smell of mortification. Only a dead preacher can give life. If a seed falls into the ground and lives, it serves only itself. But if a seed falls into the ground and dies, it becomes fruitful for others (John 12:24). Nowhere is this clearer than in Paul's explanation of how he deals with money in the ministry in 1 Corinthians 9. Let's build some context for 1 Corinthians 9, and then use it as an example of how profoundly Paul feels this idea of suffering on others' behalf.

EXPOSITION OF 1 CORINTHIANS 9

Context

The context of 1 Corinthians 9 is critical to its understanding. In chapter 8, Paul is discussing the liberty taken by the Gentile believers in their diet. Some Corinthian believers bought their meat at the market, meat that previously had been sacrificed to pagan gods. Perhaps others were eating in dining facilities closely attached to a pagan temple. These meals naturally were eaten in recognition of the bounty from the false god. Of course, this caused some spiritual dissonance, as some believers wondered how they could participate in eating food that had been dedicated to a pagan god.

Paul's chief concern in this text is the conscience of the individual believer and his or her willingness to make choices that would identify him or her with holiness before God. He goes so far as to say that the one who violates the conscience of a weaker brother is sinning against Christ. His summation of this discussion is found in 10:24–25, where he edifies them, "Let no one seek his own good, but that of his neighbor. Eat anything that is sold in the meat market without asking questions for conscience sake." So the chief consideration in their decision was to be the effect it would have on another believer. Thus, the suffering Paul experiences for them is something they should do for each other. Essentially, he was saying, "Deprive yourself of your own desires so that the gospel may live in others."

Between the discussion of personal liberty in chapter 8 and conscience in chapter 10, Paul discusses his own personal liberties to take financial provision for himself in the preaching of the gospel. The point is the same; he has the freedom, but it is a freedom he will not leverage due to a higher constraint, the sake of the gospel. Let's look at his understanding of liberty for the gospel.

He begins in verses 1 and 2 of 1 Corinthians 9 by acknowledging that he has every right to receive financial provision for the gospel: "Am I not free? Am I not an apostle? Have I not seen Jesus our Lord? Are you not my work in the Lord? If to others I am not an apostle, at least I am to you; for you are the seal of my apostleship in the Lord." Then, in verses 6 and 7, he applies the argument of personal liberty to his financial support: "Or do only Barnabas and I not have a right to refrain from working? Who at any time serves as a soldier at his own expense? Who plants a vineyard and does not eat the fruit of it? Or who tends a flock and does not use the milk of the flock?" It is very clear to Paul that he has the right to take advantage of what is his. However, he doesn't do it. The reason he does not is that he is afraid that he will be a "hindrance to the gospel" (v. 12). Paul's concern is that while he is advancing the gospel, if he takes what is rightfully his, he might keep some from the gospel.

Building a Trench

The Greek word translated "hindrance" was used in nonbiblical literature to describe the barriers armies built or the trenches they dug to provide impediments to the enemy. The Roman army especially was famous for trench building. When they would establish a camp, they would dig a trench around their camp. The dirt removed was piled behind it and held up a mobile fortress made of beams. These defenses would protect them and insulate them as they slept.[3] It is

---

3. For example, see "Roman Fortress," Exeter City Council, http://www.exeter.gov.uk/timetrail/02_romanfortress/defence.asp (accessed July 29, 2008).

this very idea that Paul uses to express his fear that the acquisition of his rights would build a barricade that was not scalable; that even if people wanted to come to the gospel, they would be prevented due to the barrier built by Paul's exercise of his rights.

Paul had been laboring among the Corinthians for quite a while, and even through all the difficulty, he had developed a deep love for them. No one could complain that Paul was not doing his work. He was not a self-absorbed slacker consumed with money. Actually, he was quite the opposite. So, outwardly at least, there was nothing to prohibit him from taking his income from those to whom he was ministering. But he doesn't do it. There was nothing wrong with it. He makes that clear. In verses 11 and 12, he writes, "If we sowed spiritual things in you, is it too much if we reap material things from you? If others share the right over you, do we not more?"

So why doesn't he take his own, well-deserved, financial support? The reason is the gospel. He is so conscious of the effects of his personal decisions on the gospel that he decides he will not, under any circumstances, do anything that will become a hindrance to the gospel. While no one would blame him for taking care of himself, he refuses, fearing he would erect a barrier to the gospel. This thought scared the brave apostle. Why would he expend himself for their lives, and at the same time build an impediment to the gospel?

Paul feared that at the same time he was drawing people to the gospel, he would be keeping them away from it. Imagine a preacher taking great pains to give his life for the gospel—investing much time and effort in education, ministry, and preaching—and yet while he does this, he builds a barrier to the gospel, a trench, an impediment.

It makes me look back over my shoulder and think about all the times I apparently extended myself for the gospel but failed to die to my personal rights. I was reaching for people and reaching for my personal comfort at the same time. While this would seem perfectly acceptable in other contexts, what I did was build a road and a trench at the same time. I was inviting people to come to a gospel they could not access due to my personal decisions. How can a man call people from danger but make it impossible to come to safety? It's not unlike yelling at the drowning to come to safety while holding them down.

This is the minister. He suspends his personal rights so that the gospel may be advanced. This suffering is the heart of the apostolic ministry. Die to *your* rights, for *their* right to hear the gospel. This is Paul's point in verse 18 when he writes, "What then is my reward? That, when I preach the gospel, I may offer the gospel without charge, so as not to make full use of my right in the gospel."

Disqualified

The end of the chapter proves quite a challenge to interpreters. Paul gives another reason that he does not take advantage of his rights. He purposefully becomes "all things to all men, so that [he] may by all means save some" (v. 22). Then he makes a provocative, often neglected, statement: "I do all things for the sake of the gospel, so that I may become a fellow partaker of it" (v. 23).

For those of us who understand the security, or the eternal preservation, of the believer as a tenant of Pauline theology, this verse seems troubling. Is Paul suggesting that his work of suffering for people in the ministry is *earning* him a place in the very gospel that he is preaching? Is he abandoning salvation by grace alone for another gospel?

It is clear that Paul advocated nothing less than grace alone for salvation; however, this provocative verse illustrates a relationship between Paul's own understanding of salvation and his suffering for others in the ministry of the gospel. This enigma is further expanded when Paul writes in verse 27, "But I discipline my body and make it my slave, so that, after I have preached to others, I myself will not be disqualified."

There are several possible interpretations of the text. However, it seems that Paul is saying God's call on his life is to suffer for others, and if he were to ever abandon this call—if he ever looked back at God and said, "No thanks, I am not interested in the gospel. I would like to go to heaven, but I no longer want to suffer for the gospel"— then he would lose the personal assurance that he was ever saved in the first place. He would not have lost something; rather, he would have proved that he never truly possessed salvation. This seems to fit the context of the passage and an interpretation of "disqualified" as meaning "proven false."[4] So Paul limits his personal freedom to illustrate to himself that he is saved. This is not about whether Paul is saved or lost. That is in the mind of God. Paul was concerned about his personal assurance of his participation in the gospel.

Thus, Paul's suffering for others increased his own personal understanding of his salvation. Paul knew he was saved by grace. However, he knew the grace was in him because of his grace-given ability to suffer for others. To reject the comforts of family life, the stability of a solitary vocation, and the ease of gentle friendships—all of these were evidence of the operative grace of God in Paul.

This helps us understand the difficult ministerial instruction given in 1 Timothy 4:16: "Pay close attention to yourself and to your teaching; persevere in these things, for as you do this you will ensure salvation both for yourself and for those who hear you." If Pauline theology demands that we understand salvation through grace alone,[5] how do we reconcile this with Paul's encouragement to Timothy?

The point seems to be similar to that in 1 Corinthians 9. The working out of the gospel in the life of the minister is so profound and real that it assures him that he is saved. Timothy is not to be assured of his salvation based on the affirmation of a creed or an emotive expression at one moment in time. He is to be assured based on the grace of God. This grace he could count on because it was operating in him, making him a faithful minister of the gospel. This became very clear as Paul wrote his "swan song" to Timothy, for Paul understood his fruitful ministry was ending and death was near.

Paul's Final Thoughts

When Paul came to the end of his life, he told his protégé Timothy, "I have fought the good fight, I have finished the course, I have kept

---

4. David Garland, *1 Corinthians*, Baker Exegetical Commentary on the New Testament (Grand Rapids: Baker, 2003), 445.

5. Cf. Romans 8:28–30; Ephesians 2:1–10.

the faith; in the future there is laid up for me the crown of righteousness, which the Lord, the righteous Judge, will award me on that day; and not only to me, but also to all who have loved his appearing" (2 Tim. 4:7–8).

There is no ministerial bravado here. This is no cocky self-assurance. Rather, this is reverential shock and awe. Despite Paul's inability to do it on his own, he *did* fight a good fight, he *did* finish the race, and he *did* keep the faith. Therefore based on his supernaturally granted ability to stay faithful to the gospel, he understands that grace is operative within him, resulting in the assurance that he truly is saved. These works did not merit salvation. They functioned to prove that salvation was indeed working in him, giving him a growing assurance that the same grace that was working in him would continue after death. Therefore the guarantee of heaven was not dependent upon his work, but rather his work was a reflection of God's grace—a grace that would continue all the way to the glorification of his body in heaven.

CONCLUSION

In all these texts it is clear that Paul understood ministry as a self-effacing deferment to the needs of others. Specifically, from 1 Corinthians 9 we understand that laying hold of personal privilege can become an impediment to the gospel. Living and dying for others was not one part of the ministry; it was a necessary means that God used to effect the salvation of others.

The question remains: Is this true of preaching? Is it true that the life-giving Word demands the death of the preacher? Is it essential that the preacher suffer so that the people will not suffer? Paul answers this question in 1 Corinthians 2:1–5, perhaps the clearest statement on preaching in the New Testament.

[2]

Dying So Others Might Live (Part 2)

The Cross in the Pulpit

It is clear that the idea of suffering for others is not a passing thought in Paul's ministry. This is the cord that binds his ministry together. It is not peripheral. It is essential. This is the vibrant aspect of Paul's ministry. The centrality of his suffering for the Corinthians infused everything he did for them. It was so central to his understanding of ministry that one could argue that he believed it essential to ministry. To say it explicitly, Paul believed that their spiritual life depended upon his death to himself. If he did not die, they would not live.

If this is true for ministry generally, it is certainly true of preaching in particular. In fact, 1 Corinthians 2:1–5 applies the idea of living and dying for others specifically to preaching. There is more written on this text than can be imagined, but the modest treatment here is intended to illustrate that Paul understood his preaching ministry as suffering for the people.

EXPOSITION OF 1 CORINTHIANS 2:1–5

And when I came to you, brethren, I did not come with superiority of speech or of wisdom, proclaiming to you the testimony of God. For I determined to know nothing among you except Jesus Christ, and Him crucified. I was with you in weakness and in fear and in much trembling, and my message and my preaching were not in persuasive words of wisdom, but in demonstration of the Spirit and of power, so that your faith would not rest on the wisdom of men, but on the power of God.

As Paul began his ministry in Corinth, it was not without difficulty. As mentioned earlier, this was one challenging church. In fact, the very reason Paul wrote his first letter was in response to a fight in the church. All the licentiousness in the church was compounded by division in the ranks. It seems that even those willing to follow the teachings of Christ were divided into camps based on what leader they followed.

In the first chapter Paul writes that some said they were of Paul, and others of Apollos, and others of Cephas. Some have suggested that this early division in the church was even a division over preaching.[1] This is an interesting suggestion. Here is Paul, the heady, left-brained theologian, the guy who is all substance and no style, giving out challenging exhortations with theological precision and cogent insight. By his own admission, Paul was not that great a communicator. Perhaps he made it on his intellect alone. One can imagine that due to Paul's scintillating intellect he drew quite a following among the Corinthian church. Yet, it is also plausible that some may not have liked his approach, that some found his logic hard to follow. Why did he have to speak in such harsh tones without the polish of the modern-day orator? Why couldn't Paul be slick and easy to listen to, and why did he refuse to preach in a way that they liked and to which they were accustomed?

Well, for those people, there was Apollos. Acts 18:24 speaks of Apollos as *aner logios*, a man who was eloquent. Perhaps there was a group of people attracted to Apollos precisely because of his communication ability. Can you imagine them thinking, "Don't give me

1. See Michael Bullmore, *St. Paul's Theology of Rhetorical Style: An Examination of 1 Corinthians 2:1–5 in Light of First Century Graeco-Roman Rhetorical Culture* (San Francisco: International Scholars Publications, 1995).

Paul with his heady theological diatribes. Give me the fascinating communication of Apollos. I can listen to him preach all day!" While we cannot know for certain, it would be very interesting to know if part of the dissension in Corinth was over the style of preaching of its leaders.

Whatever the reason, it drove the apostle to launch into a discussion of his understanding of preaching. He observes in 1 Corinthians 1:27–28 that "God has chosen the weak things of the world to shame the things which are strong, and the base things of the world and the despised God has chosen, the things that are not, so that He may nullify the things that are."

In sum, God specifically has chosen the foolishness of preaching to be the instrument by which He saves those who believe. This choice had the double purpose of drawing those who believed and illustrating God's power by accomplishing His purposes through that which is debased in the eyes of those who consider themselves wise.

The context of this discussion is interesting since Paul is writing to those influenced by the "wisdom" of the Hellenistic world. He is setting them up for his seminal passage on his preaching philosophy. He has just dealt with God's purpose of preaching in chapter 1, and now he will explain why he does what he does, and how he does it.

First, Paul says that he does not come to them with "superiority of speech or of wisdom" (1 Cor. 2:1). This is an odd confession. After all, Paul is veraciously wise. His intellect is profound and his wit inestimable. So why did he say that in his preaching, in his "proclaiming," he did not come with superior speech?

It is clear that this is an extension of his initial argument posed in 1:17, where he writes, "For Christ did not send me to baptize, but to preach the gospel, not in cleverness of speech, so that the cross of Christ would not be made void." Paul is stating that a preached message filled with "cleverness of speech" would nullify the gospel. So he opts to keep the message simple—a pure gospel, a gospel not adulterated with a false sense of wisdom.

Paul's aim for the purity of the gospel message, while very clear, does not help us answer our question. If Paul is not using wisdom or superior speech, how do we explain this brilliantly composed argument to Corinth? How do we explain his quotation of Athenian poets in Acts 17, his use of rhetorical device in Romans 6:1, or his breathtaking Christological passages in Philippians 2 and Colossians 1? For that matter, how can we explain the entire book of Romans? Paul *was* wise, his speech *was* superior, and he *was* indeed a brilliant intellect who took advantage of classical rhetorical devices in his writings and sermons. So again, where does he find the nerve to say that he did not come to the Corinthians with wisdom or superior speech? The answer may lie in an understanding of what he meant by "wisdom" and "superior speech."

Superiority of Speech and Wisdom

It is hard to imagine today, but in ancient Corinth, listening to speeches was a popular form of entertainment. The effective orator, therefore, was well respected in the culture. In fact, a sophistic communicator could find himself a very wealthy man. He was often a hired gun, who would sell his skills to the highest payer to defend a client, put forth a general idea, or persuade the populace. Without electronic communication, this was as good as it got.

Sitting down and listening to a brilliant speechmaker would put a common person in awe of the speaker's ability to perform rhetorical gymnastics. While this was a noble profession, it often was marked by abuse. There were the Sophists, who, with some notable exceptions, simply made speeches for the sake of it. The content was arbitrary, as their goal was to turn every imaginable rhetorical flourish, weave any verbal trick, and hold the audience within the palm of their hand with emotional manipulation. They were all style and no substance. They were communicators with nothing to communicate, and therefore they themselves became the message. The point of their speech was essentially, "See how great a speech I can make."

In fact, it is safe to assume that the Corinthians would have known exactly what Paul was talking about when he used the expression "superior speech." The Corinthians would have been exposed to some phenomenal communicators. It is widely held that the Corinthians, influenced by Cicero, would have been aware of fascinating orators who could hold an audience with their amazing communication abilities. These men came to prominence with a style that easily would have been identified by Paul's audience. So perhaps Paul was referring to a classical form of Greco-Roman rhetoric, a rhetoric for which the Corinthians had developed an appetite—a kind that perhaps they loved. So Paul is not suggesting that all rhetoric is bad or that his personal speech was not good; he is suggesting that the kind of speech he chose was not filled with the over-the-top rhetorical tricks with which the Corinthians were so familiar. His sermons were not filled with language that was far above their heads.[2] Instead, Paul opted for the simplicity of coming to them with Jesus alone.

Knowing Nothing

Verse 2 is so familiar it is easy to miss its implications. Paul decided "to know nothing among [the Corinthians] except Jesus Christ, and Him crucified." While the texts we dealt with in chapter 1 spoke of Paul's physical suffering for the Corinthians, here he speaks of his intellectual challenges. Paul was schooled under Gamaliel. He was an expert in Jewish law, a Hebrew of the Hebrews, and a man who by lineage and by education was intellectually elite. Yet he said that his one ambition among them was to know nothing but the simplicity of the gospel. This deference to their needs is instructive. It was not his ambition for the Corinthians to know how much he knew. That was beside the point. His ambition was for them to know Christ alone.

The "nothing" of verse 2 was exactly the wisdom to which he had been referring. Paul determined to preach the simplicity of the gospel among the Corinthians. This text shames me. How many times have I entered the pulpit, and deep within my heart, in a place too hidden to be obvious, was a secret desire for everyone to know just how much

---

2. David Garland, *1 Corinthians*, Baker Exegetical Commentary on the New Testament (Grand Rapids: Baker, 2003), 82.

I knew, for the audience to pine over my sensibilities about modern culture, observations from everyday life, and ability to explain the sacred text. The truth is that this "hidden" desire is obvious to people. They know if we are preaching to hear ourselves talk or being a manifestation of the Word of God so that it can reveal the Word who is God. Paul's point is a convicting one. In style and in content, he was determined to communicate nothing less than the purity of the gospel message.

Persuasive Words of Wisdom

Then, in verse 3 Paul echoes the sentiment of verse 5 by contrasting his choice of communication style with what he did not choose. Paul says that he intentionally did not come in "persuasive words of wisdom," again a reference to a style of communication with which the Corinthians would have been familiar. This is a fascinating verse and perhaps the most poignant discussion of preaching style in the New Testament.

Preaching style grabs a lot of attention these days. Just as we have defined our worship music by style (traditional, contemporary, emergent, etc.), we have defined our preaching. There is a host of literature telling the preacher how he can find a style that best reflects the culture of the audience and use that style to effectively communicate with the audience. It makes sense. However, here Paul is saying, "Look, I know exactly the kind of style that you like, and I am intentionally not using it." This is odd. Why would any effective communicator, after effectively exegeting his audience and identifying the style they like, *not* use it? The answer for Paul is very simple: he is driven by fear.

Paul's fear is that if he so closely identified his preaching with the expected Greco-Roman forms, they might like it. In fact, they might like it so much that they might understand his style as foundational to their faith. His desire was that their "faith would not rest on the wisdom of men, but on the power of God" (v. 5). The liability of a presumptuous style of preaching, no matter how well intended, is misplaced faith. The preacher preaches a phenomenal message, and the people have a wonderful response. They leave enthralled with the preacher and impressed by the sermon, but their faith is in the preacher and not the gospel. Before further discussion of Paul, let's make some application to our contemporary setting.

THE MEDIUM IS ULTIMATE

It could be argued that today the style of preaching has become more important than its substance. Those who study communication have long been interested in the relationship between the style and the substance of communication and their related impact on the communication act.

Rhetorical theorist and student of 1960s pop culture Marshall McLuhan was best known for the phrase "the medium is the message."[3] McLuhan's overstatement was intended to illustrate the impact that certain modes of communication have on their content. For example, the messages *from* television are necessarily altered by the fact that they are *on* television. A story told on television takes a totally different shape, simply because of the medium of television. The visual story, which comes to us by waves traveling through the air and is then reproduced on a little monitor, is different than if told orally or in a live performance. The medium of TV forces the storyteller to tell it in a different way. McLuhan argues that this alteration of the story's substance, to accommodate the medium of the story, is so profound that the medium is in fact the story itself. In this example the medium (television) has become the message (an altered story).

McLuhan also said that "we shape the tools and the tools shape us."[4] For example, man invented television, but it is interesting to note how many lives are ruled by its programming. Man invented computers and is now dependent upon them for survival. (Before you

---

3. McLuhan also was famous as a "technological determinist," wordsmith, and scholar. His book *The Medium Is the Massage* played on the way that media "massages" the listener and the fact that we are living in the mass-age. For a concise look at McLuhan, see www.marshallmacluhan.com.
4. For an accessible treatment of McLuhan's life and influence, see http://www.regent.edu/acad/schcom/rojc/mdic/McLuhan.html.

call this an overstatement, remember the Y2K rations that were in your basement.)

All theory aside, we know intuitively that the message of television is not to buy a certain product or even to be entertained; rather, the message of television is television itself. It is its most important product to promote. In other words, television exists to promote more watching of television. The medium (bits of information on a screen) is the message. We understand that television does not enhance our lives nearly as much as it compels us to watch more television. The medium is the message.

Make no mistake about it—preaching is a powerful medium. Think about it. Here you are with a congregation of people in front of you—some are facing God's judgment for their sin and don't even know it, while still others have at best a warped sense of Christianity. All that stands between you and this gathered crowd is a book. And you stand, like it or not, as an authority on that Book, telling them what God says about ultimate questions.

The fact that you are standing before people with the Word of God in front of you screams several things before you even open your mouth. First, you are communicating that you are the authority for the moment. Second, the medium communicates that God has spoken to you directly as to what you are to say. Third, the medium of preaching communicates that by virtue of calling, appointment, or sheer nerve for all your listeners know, you have postured yourselves to speak to the deepest needs of the heart.

It is clear that the medium of preaching is certainly a message in itself. Here's the rub. *The preacher who is not disgusted with the flesh and filled with a healthy fear of God's judgment will allow the medium to be the primary message.* The sermon need not necessarily communicate the text clearly, for the crowd that recognizes that the preaching of the sermon is actually its message will be completely satisfied with a sermon that sounds like a sermon, a sermon that can mildly entertain them and is delivered by a preacher who looks like a preacher. In this scenario the *medium of preaching has replaced the substance of the sermon.* The style of the sermon has eclipsed what the scriptural text is saying. The medium of preaching has become the message of the sermon.

I know this because I have done it. I have received praise for average sermons from friends who could not, or refused to, acknowledge the fact that my raised voice and attempts at humor veiled a poor exposition and poor preparation. How in God's name (literally) could I get away with this? If the preacher does not clearly explain Scripture, would not someone stand up and say, "Where's the point? Where are you going with this?" or more aptly, "What did you do between Sundays?" However, rarely does the preacher worry about such a response because the medium of preaching has become its message. The truth is that low expectations are rarely disappointed. Expecting no more, the people are saying that the medium is enough. The congregation is satisfied with one who looks like, acts like, and sounds like a preacher, even if the message of preaching is secondary to its medium.

What is most peculiar is that no one thinks this is peculiar. How could this happen? How could people be satisfied with the medium of preaching when the message is not strong? The answer may lie in the fact that, again, the medium of preaching is indeed a profound medium and a wonderful art—an art that, as we will see, is at once powerful and persuasive.

THE PERSUASIVE ART

In the sixteenth century, Francois Fénelon, going even further than McLuhan, made the observation that all art is inherently persuasive.[5] He argued that even the most passive pieces of art persuade one to have a certain mood, to do or to feel something. The art may even be persuading one not to change moods or feelings. However, one cannot see a painting, hear a song, or read a book without being persuaded in some way.

The great example of art as persuasion is music. Some songs affect

5. Wilbur Samuel Howell, "Oratory and Poetry in Fénelon's Literary Theory," *Quarterly Journal of Speech* 37 (1951): 1–10.

us in powerful ways, like an Irishman listening to "Danny Boy" or a University of Alabama football fan listening to the Crimson Tide fight song. Some songs persuade us in subtle ways. The background music in a department store is composed and performed in a way that evokes a certain feeling in the listener. We could go on, but it is clear that art *is* persuasive, even if the persuasion is subtle and even if it is unintentional. Therefore, if preaching is an art, then the preaching act *itself* is persuasive. If the congregation is captivated by a sermon from a passionate preacher, they are persuaded to do what God, through the preacher, is calling them to do. If the listeners are bored, then perhaps they are persuaded to suspect the profound irrelevance of God to their lives. If preaching is art, and all art is persuasive, then every sermon persuades to something—even if it is not what the preacher intended. The listener may be persuaded toward radical life change, to momentary contrition, to think well of the preacher, or to never return to church. Preaching cannot exist in a vacuum of persuasion.

The point is that since all preaching is persuasive, the preacher must decide to what he will persuade his audience or, more precisely, to whom he will persuade his audience. The preacher who is not passionate about the text he is preaching, or the God of the text, becomes himself the object of the persuasion. This is the temptation of all preaching.

THE TEMPTATION

If you think I am exaggerating the point for emphasis, try preaching a great message while changing the medium. Your illustrations are clear, your exposition is precise, and your application is helpful. Just change one thing—the medium. Skip the tie or the robe, and preach in an Oriental kimono. Then preach the highest quality sermon you have ever preached. You will probably discover that you have not been heard. Why? The message inherent in the medium is so deafening that your words cannot be heard. One quickly discovers that McLuhan is at least partially right—the medium is the message. We also discover that Fénelon is right—the art, in its presentation, is persuasive. *Thus, there exists the temptation to hone and master the preaching medium to the point that we, and consequently the congregation, are unaware that the medium of preaching not only has become a part of the message, but also has trumped the message of Scripture itself.* More precisely, the medium of preaching has replaced the message of the gospel.

DEFINED BY STYLE

Throughout history churches have multiplied and divided under certain theological designations. Words like *liberal, Reformed, evangelical, moderate, conservative,* or *fundamentalist* have all been used to define the substance of the church. However, when identifying an evangelical church in the twenty-first century, rarely are these substance words a consideration. Denominational identification is even less important. In fact, it could be argued that this is the first generation of evangelical churches to define themselves primarily by style. While this is a mild overstatement, it is often true that the designations for a church are not substance words but style words such as *traditional* or *contemporary.*[6] These are not words used to describe the substance of a church's beliefs; rather, they describe its style. Naturally, when we define our churches by style, we are generally referring to the style of the church's corporate worship, including the sermon. Now, let's think about the potential implications of this style identity on the sermon itself.

Think about the temptation a pastor in a contemporary worship context faces. The preacher, and thus the sermon, is expected to be— often above all else—contemporary. If his sermon is trendy, his illustrations relevant, his dress appealing, and his props engaging, then that style, not the Scripture, could become the primary message. The irony is that in the same way the traditional pastor is bound by his traditional style, the contemporary pastor, perhaps in a reach for freedom in worship, is bound by his contemporary style.

The traditional preacher faces the same temptation. He can shape

---

6. These are obviously elastic, popular terms that are used mostly as designations for corporate worship. Their inherent limitation is that they mean many different things to different groups. The terms are used broadly here for the purpose of illustration.

the form of a sermon in such a way that over time the form—the vocal tone, pitch, alliteration, use of illustration—becomes more important to the hearers than the message. His communication style trains the hearer to listen for style above substance. The result is the creation of false boundaries. These boundaries lead the listener to evaluate the sermon on its adherence to the means rather than on the message itself. The point here is not to criticize one style over another. The point is that if we define our worship ultimately by style, logic dictates that preaching, as an act of worship, must be defined by style. If we define our preaching by style exclusively, let us be honest enough to say that style, above all else, often becomes *the* defining test of preaching. The medium is the message. God help us for reducing this most important task, communicating His Word, to an argument over style.

Is style important? Of course. Often in church growth circles, we hear the phrase "change the method, not the message." That is sage advice. The elastic methods will, and should, envelope the unchanging message.

But honestly, not every method is conducive to every message. Neil Postman effectively argues that much of television preaching is light and trivial. This is not because the gospel message is light but because the medium of television itself is light and trivial. Postman writes, "I believe I am not mistaken in saying that Christianity is a demanding and serious religion. When it is delivered as easy and amusing, it is another kind of religion altogether."[7]

In other words, some have allowed the medium of television to change the message of the gospel. To say it another way, when the context of preaching is more important than the content of preaching, then the context (medium) becomes the content (message) itself.

It is important to remember that this can happen in any tradition: with the preacher who is expected to yell to be effective, the preacher who is expected to be mild to be effective, the preacher who is expected to be inoffensive, the preacher who is expected to be contemporary, or the preacher who is expected to be polished to be effective.

---

7. Neil Postman, *Amusing Ourselves to Death* (New York: Penguin, 1992), 121.

The temptation for style to trump substance is not limited to any particular tradition or style.

In any approach or style, the message can move from God's Word to "My preaching is holding up a tradition" or "My preaching is reacting against a tradition." It is true that preaching will always reflect the preacher's style and personality. However, who he is, is not the message. The medium is important, but it is secondary to the message. Whatever the chosen medium, gut-level honesty demands that we admit that too often we have made style the arbiter of effective preaching.

SO WHAT?

So what if style is an issue? After all, God created us as a diverse people with a desire for diversity, so our preaching should reflect this reality. Individuals like certain styles, and that should not matter. Agreed. There are some styles that really work with me personally. They just move me more than others. No doubt there are great students of Scripture who could greatly extend their preaching ministry if they would give more attention to their sermon delivery. Style of delivery is not unimportant.

However, at this point I have wanted to suggest only that (1) it is possible that we have defined preaching ultimately by style, and (2) by saying that style is ultimate, we have errantly taught our congregations to value the medium of preaching over the message of the Scripture. Yet, one still might ask, "If this is true, then so what?" After all, preaching done well, as defined by style, is better than preaching with a poor style! This is true. However, as we will see, Paul suggests in 1 Corinthians 2:1–5 that *an obsession with style will actually be counterproductive to the gospel message.* What damnable irony. We work to make the message great in order to reach people, and in reality we produce people who know when they have heard a "good sermon," but do not know the gospel. They have a highly realized sense of sermon critique but are apathetic, lazy, and indifferent to the gospel.

So Paul dies to the idea of ever being thought of as a great communicator, even though it seems he had it in him. It seems that the skill set to be a great communicator was imbedded in the apostle, but he chose otherwise. His reputation for communicating the gospel was far less important than the fact that it was communicated.

It is at this point that Paul's words about suffering for his people intersect with preaching. For a preacher to die, he must die to his right to be thought of as a great preacher. For the Word of God to live in people, the preacher must die to his right to be thought of as a great preacher. He must embrace the reality that what people need the most will not always be what they want to hear.

I am not advocating misunderstanding our culture, or living aloof to the world around us. This would be just as sinful as the other extreme. The vice that this text exposes in me is being so familiar with the rhetorical buttons that I can push that I groom people to fall in love with sermons and not Christ. This reminds me of the old joke about the soldier who wrote home every day, for a full year, to his girlfriend. After receiving over three hundred letters, she fell in love with the postman.

So here I stand in the pulpit with a love letter. My responsibility is to deliver the letter so that the intended recipients can understand, on a profound level, the deep mystery of the Father's love for them. They are not supposed to fall in love with the postman. I must never use the Word of God in an insecure attempt to garner personal affection for myself. Yet this temptation is so subtle that it seems impossible not to do it. But think how twisted it is to take the very words of God and manipulate them to fulfill narcissistic ends. Sometimes I am too stubborn, too blind, or just too pious to admit that I do this. It's at those times I have to ask:

- Have I ever manipulated a text to fit an imposed outline?
- Have I ever neglected a text of Scripture because it would cause people to think of me poorly?
- Have I ever "glossed" a difficult passage in order to maintain a sermon's flow or style?

- Have I neglected to preach the difficult themes of Scripture?
- Have I ever approached Scripture looking for a sermon, instead of asking God, "What is it that You want to say to Your love interest in this text?"
- Have I ever twisted a text in order to fit an illustration or a prop?
- Have I considered the need of God to communicate and the need of people to hear less important than my desire to be liked?
- Have I ever preached sermons that exalted man as the center and God as marginal?
- Does my preaching calendar celebrate cultural holidays more than the death, burial, and resurrection of Christ?

Make no mistake, the preacher himself is the love interest of Christ as well. However, knowing this love, we imitate Christ who, motivated by the love of the Father, enveloped Himself in flesh, was delivered to the world as a gift, and lived a life that allowed us to read the love letter of God to us. In this way He is the Word that we hear telling us of the love of the Father for us.

The purpose of preaching is not more preaching; the purpose of preaching is the exaltation of Christ through His Word. My fear is that my preaching will groom a generation of pew sitters, perfectly skilled to recognize a gem when they hear it but still ignorant of what God says, not filled with a sense of the pressing impetus on them to obey the Word. This is the kind of preaching that builds churches but does not make disciples. The people become window gazers who have not been taught to gaze at the life-giving words. Preaching is medicine first and art second.

The reason this is so critical is the theological liability that is attached to it. Paul said that if he made preaching about himself, if his sermons became the message and not the medium, his listeners' faith would be displaced—from faith in God to faith in the preacher. The temptation is to succumb to the waves of temptation that lap up on our boat, to simply be carried away in the predictable pattern of self-serving preaching week after week. The people in the boat with us are not strong enough to swim. So if we are not faithful to preach texts of Scripture, they might drown in their appreciation for our ability, while never being brought safely to the shore of salvation. The risk is huge. This is actually the point that Paul tries to make in 2 Corinthians 4.

Here's the bottom line. If we look at the church today, it is pretty clear that the masses are not following the pattern of discipleship found in the New Testament. We know this. We talk about this. We write about this. Perhaps we talk about it so much that it has lost its shock value. Think of the problem this way: The church of Jesus Christ does not love Jesus Christ *through the Word*. The place they learned that they could have a Christianity void of a passion for Scripture is from us, from the preachers, from me. We can bemoan the lethargic state of the church. We can preach about it and call for revival. We can talk about the glory of God and the exaltation of Christ. However, we cannot complain when our people do what we model. Or, more precisely, how can we blame people when they live like we preach, without deference to the authority of God's Word in all things? Eventually, the pew is the mirror of the pulpit. There will be no sustained life change in people until pastors give themselves to teaching people Scripture. Perhaps the next big conference topic should be the lack of need for more conferences and the real need for more accountability for us to simply preach Scripture.

It is pretty obvious that Paul is borrowing this idea of suffering from the very atonement of Christ Himself. And as we further read the Scriptures, it becomes clear that the idea of surrender, of a death so that others can live, is so closely tied to the sufferings of Christ that the preacher is actually participating in the suffering of Christ when he chooses to die so that his people may live.

So the question remains, what does this mean for preaching? As we read through the New Testament, this is worked out in at least four ways that apply to the contemporary preacher. If preaching is dying so that others may live, then

1. we must suffer to get the text clear so that the light of Christ can flow through us to ignite the human heart (2 Cor. 4:1–6);
2. we must suffer to invite people to the center of everything, which is Christ (Col. 1:24);
3. we must identify with Christ and His suffering (Heb. 13:10–14);
4. we must imitate Christ's surrender to the will of the Father, in the same way that He died so that others could live (Phil. 2:1–6). For this reason we surrender ourselves to the Word of God, to the audience, and to excellence in preaching.

Therefore we must understand the cross, we must understand the pulpit, and we must understand the cross in the pulpit. Think of it as the event of the cross, layered over the event of the pulpit . . .

THE CROSS

Jesus walks into Jerusalem. Like no one else He knows what awaits Him there. So in Gethsemane He falls on His face. The task is too great, and in a moment of writhing transparency, He buries His knees in the dirt, clasps His rugged hands, looks up to heaven, and begs His Father to remove the cup of wrath from the table of tomorrow. If there were another way than to take up that biting chalice, He would take it. Heaven is silent, and He knows what He must do. So He stands up and walks away, so thirsty for the Father's pleasure that He drinks the cup of His wrath for others. Only the grace of the Father can sustain Him, and this is why He prays. But tonight He feels so alone. This is not a light cross. He can't run. He must bear it. And He must bear it alone.

So He allows Himself to be stripped of all that is dignified, of all that is attractive. He willingly puts Himself in the most vulnerable position. Seeing the faces of those who torture Him, He remains undaunted. Falling to the ground under the weight of the cross, He lifts His corpus off the ground and rises to communicate God's love. Then He stretches out His hands, and He dies. In a thousand ways He wants this to end, but He stays. And as life is being drained from Him, there is something taking place that no one else can see. From eternity past to eternity present, sins are being forgiven, debts are being cleared; atonement, sweet atonement is being accomplished. From all the putrid stench of hell, from all the wickedness of Satan's bastard children, up from the grotesque composite of trillions of sins, the ravishing Lily of the Valley is in full bloom. Life has come. So He screams the conclusion of this homily of heaven and hell from the pulpit of His cross, "It is finished!" And soon that buried life will rise again to prove that the spiritual reality is a physical one. Life from death. Death for Life. The exchange produces the pardon of sin. Oh the sweet vicarious suffering of Jesus that won us our salvation!

THE PULPIT

The preacher stares coldly at the blank screen in front of him and the Bible beside him. He would never admit it, but this process has always scared him. To some it might come easy, but not for him. He is not at all sure that he understands what this text means. He really wants the people to know God but he just can't get past the confusing nature of the Bible. A thousand shortcuts are at his disposal. He can borrow the whole thing. He can look at the commentaries while he is reading the text, even before he is reading the text. Any option is more attractive than studying this thing deeply until he has the meaning in his gut.

However, he decides to do it. He decides to exchange his effort to be used of God for their sanctification. He is weighted down with the gravity of the lost people who will be listening to him. He wrestles with the text and ponders its meaning. And slowly the Holy Spirit of God drives the text into his heart. His flesh is wounded. He knows he must repent. And just the time that he thinks he will never get the meaning, the light of understanding awakens his mind to spiritual truth. Continually bathing this whole matter in prayer, he gets up from his knees.

On Sunday, he lifts his corpus from the chair and moves to confront the people. Stares of dispassionate lethargy meet him; he wonders if this will do anything. Will it communicate? This room represents his closest fellowship, yet this is the lonely place, the place where he portends to do God's work. Will the text be clear? Since he cannot answer these questions, he just keeps preaching. And he gives his life in those moments. Pulsating with every heartbeat, the light of the Word pours through him and onto the people. Every word is a prayer that God will bring light from their darkness. In his heart he wants to stop and draw the attention to himself, to shade the truth to make himself look better, to tell that story that will take the edge off the bite of the text and give his friends a way out. But if his wit, his humor, and his intellect live in this way, the people will die spiritually. So he stays tethered to the text. Then it happens. He can sense that the Word of God is penetrating the darkness, and the Son of God, as revealed from the Word, is rising in the hearts of people. So he appeals for God's people to submit to God's revelation of Himself, and he sits down. He waits. Later, the hardened face of a sinner is before him, and he can see it. Christ has revealed Himself in the Word and saved this one. The darkness lays pitifully at his feet in a thousand pieces. Sweet atonement! The sinner is pardoned and free. God brought life. God brought life from death. God brought life from death at the price of the preacher's death in the pulpit.

THE PULPIT OF THE CROSS / THE CROSS OF THE PULPIT

Jesus walks into Jerusalem. Like no one else, he knows what awaits him there. So he stares coldly at the blank screen. A thousand shortcuts are at his disposal. He can borrow the whole thing. He can forge his own ideas on the anvil of his insight and impose them on the text. He can look at the commentaries while he is reading the text, even before he is reading the text. Any option is more attractive than studying this thing deeply until he has the meaning in his gut.

And in that moment, he cannot find any other way to handle this situation but to simply know God through His Word so he can lead others to do the same. So he stands up and walks away, so thirsty for the Father's pleasure that he decides to die so that others may live. Only the grace of the Father can sustain him, and this is why he prays. This is not a light cross. He can't run. He must bear it. And he must bear it alone.

So he allows himself to be stripped of all that is dignified, of all that is attractive. He willingly puts himself in the most vulnerable position. He knows that God wants to make these people like Him, so he will have to do it. Stares of dispassionate lethargy meet him; he wonders if this will do anything. Will it communicate? Will the text be clear? Since he cannot answer these questions, he just keeps preaching. Then he stretches out his hands, and he dies. In a thousand ways he wants this to end, but he stays. And as the life is flowing from him, there is something taking place that no one else can see. From eternity past to eternity present, sins are being forgiven, debts are being cleared, atonement, sweet atonement, is being accomplished. From all the putrid stench of hell, from all the wickedness of Satan's bastard children, up from the grotesque composite of trillions of sins, the Lily of the Valley is in full bloom. Life has come.

So he screams the conclusion of this homily of heaven and hell from the pulpit of his cross, "It is finished!" And as he reaches his conclusion and appeals for God's people to submit to God's revelation of Himself, he comes down and waits. Later, the hardened face of a sinner is before him, and he can see it. Sweet atonement! The sinner is pardoned and free. God brought life. God brought life from death. God brought life from death at the price of the death of His Son, extended in his death in the pulpit. The exchange of Christ's life for the sinner produces the pardon of sin. Oh the sweet vicarious suffering of Jesus that won us our salvation!

Part 2

Four Implications of the Cross in the Pulpit

The following section explores the implications of the cross in the pulpit from four texts. The cross in the pulpit is God's means of igniting the human heart (2 Cor. 4:1–6). It is also the means by which we invite others to him by the extension of the sufferings of Christ (Col. 1:24). We are commanded to identify with the cross by bearing the reproach of the cross in our preaching (Heb. 13:10–14). Finally, we are called to imitate Christ in His selfless deference to sinful people above His own desires (Phil. 2:5–11).

[3]

Ignite

Preaching the Cross of Christ

Since only Christ can ignite the human heart, preachers must not preach themselves but only the word that
reveals Christ, who is the image of the Father.

*Therefore, since we have this ministry, as we received mercy,
we do not lose heart, but we have renounced the things hidden because of shame, not walking in craftiness or adulter-
ating the word of God, but by the manifestation of truth
commending ourselves to every man's conscience in the sight
of God. And even if our gospel is veiled, it is veiled to those
who are perishing, in whose case the god of this world has
blinded the minds of the unbelieving so they might not see the
light of the gospel of the glory of Christ, who is the image of
God. . . . For God, who said, "Light shall shine out of darkness," is the One who has shone in our hearts to give the Light
of the knowledge of the glory of God in the face of Christ.*
—2 Corinthians 4:1–4, 6

As I teach preaching, I can see the struggle in the eyes of the students. Perhaps they are trying to figure out with whom they will
identify themselves in ministry. Will they be traditional, seeker, or
emergent in their orientation? The temptation of course is to ask the

style question first: What style of preacher will I be? Or more specifically, what style of delivery will I use? These are not bad questions really. It is better to choose your friends than to have them chosen for you. However, it's not the first question that should be asked. But this concern over style is a learned behavior. Often students are asking the style question because they have been taught, at least by imitation, that this *is* the first question.

Sometimes a student will ask if I believe the expository *style* of preaching is the only way to go since that is what we teach at our seminary. I do not. I do not believe that expository style should be understood as the only way to preach because exposition is not a style per se. It may seem like splitting hairs, but think about it. If someone believes that exposition is the only style, and by exposition the person means a specific stylized sermonic structure (i.e., three or four points, an introduction, and a conclusion), then I could not defend that structural style as the only way to go. This is not because I do not have a high view of Scripture; rather, this is precisely because I have too high a view of Scripture to take the precious Word of God, with its multiple genres that God inspired to communicate Himself, and force it to fit a predetermined outline. My fear is that many who work to honor the text miss the true impact of a text because they do not honor the rhetorical structure of a passage. The problem, of course, is that there is not only meaning at the substance level (word studies, biblical theology, etc.), but there is also meaning at the structural level, and the spirit level. So if God inspired a story (which has no "points," only scenes), or a poem, or law, or history, then should not those structures influence our preaching? In other words, shouldn't the structure of the text determine the structure of the sermon?[1]

So we teach text-driven preaching; that is, preaching where the

---

1. For a helpful discussion of preaching the genres of Scripture, see Jeffrey Arthurs, *Preaching with Variety: How to Re-create the Dynamics of Biblical Genres* (Grand Rapids: Kregel, 2007). For a discussion of honoring the genre of the Old Testament narratives, see Stephen D. Mathewson, *The Art of Preaching Old Testament Narrative* (Grand Rapids: Baker, 2002).

text determines not only the subject of the sermon but its structure and spirit as well. We often call this exposition, but in reference to the philosophy, not the style per se. *Expository preaching, or text-driven preaching, is not a style; rather, it is a theologically driven philosophy of preaching.* Style is the last question someone should ask. A question that must precede it is: What is my philosophy of preaching?

There are other philosophies of preaching. Some prefer topical preaching, in which a biblical topic or a cultural topic drives the sermon. Others prefer what I refer to as a text-centered sermon. This is where all the points come from a given text, even though the sermon may not honor the structure of the text, the spirit of the text, or even the subject of the text. For example, I once heard a text-centered sermon on tithing from John 3:16. The idea of the sermon was "God so loved the world that He gave—so dig deep!" The preacher may argue that his point of tithing came from the text. While it is true that John 3:16 is about giving, it is about what God gave, not our financial sacrifices. Some might respond, "What's the big deal? We do need to give, and God gave; so why not connect the dots?" The problem with this approach is that everything we say in the pulpit we say to the exclusion of something else. So while you could preach this sermon without being heretical, you will miss the glorious truth of God's sacrifice for us in the atonement of Christ! That's the big deal.

There is a relationship between the atonement and giving found in 2 Corinthians 9, and it would be fair to preach it from that text. Perhaps much that goes under the name "expository preaching" is more accurately text-centered preaching—preaching that finds its points in a text without consideration of the context, genre, or the true authorial intent of the text. However, it is still referred to as expository because it imitates an expositional style. We cannot excuse ourselves from faithfully preaching the text because we have followed the style of another preacher who does follow the text. Imitation of others is not license to preach beyond the limits of a text. So while philosophy of preaching is very important, it's just not the first question we should ask.

PAUL'S THEOLOGY OF COMMUNICATION

The first question is not about how we structure sermons (philosophy) or the method of delivery (style). The first question should be the theology question: *What is it about the nature of God's communication that demands that we communicate in a certain way?* We can then ask the second question, the question of philosophy: What approach to preaching best accomplishes that aim? The last question is: What style of delivery should we employ? This last question will be determined largely by our context and personality and is usually answered once we have answered the first two questions.

Figure 1.

Theology	God has revealed Himself through Christ, and Christ through the Word
Philosophies	Text-Driven Text-Centered Topical
Styles of Delivery	Emergent Traditional Seeker

As a professor I understand that I have one shot to get a student to embrace the idea that the Communicator can determine how He wants to be communicated. To say it more specifically, there is something about God's revelation of Himself that puts boundaries on my communication. Paul seemed convinced that how God communicated Himself determines how we are to communicate God. In this way the subject of communication dictates the way it is communicated. Please read carefully as Paul's words serve as the template for the cross in the pulpit.

EXPOSITION OF 2 CORINTHIANS 4:1-6

In 2 Corinthians 4:11–12 Paul gives the seminal statement on suffering on others' behalf in ministry: "For we who live are constantly being delivered over to death for Jesus' sake, so that the life of Jesus also may be manifested in our mortal flesh. So death works in us, but life in you." Paul is very clear that the life that needs to be imbedded in the life of the people is contingent upon his personal death.

Arguably, the quintessential explanation of Paul's own ministry is found in 2 Corinthians 4:1–6:

> Therefore since we have this ministry, as we have received mercy, we do not lose heart, but we have renounced the things hidden because of shame, not walking in craftiness or adulterating the word of God, but by the manifestation of truth commending ourselves to every man's conscience in the sight of God. And even if our gospel is veiled, it is veiled to those who are perishing, in whose case the god of this world has blinded the minds of the unbelieving so they might not see the light of the gospel of the glory of Christ, who is the image of God. *For we do not preach ourselves* but Christ Jesus as Lord, and ourselves as your bond-servants for Jesus' sake. For God, who said, "Light shall shine out of darkness," is the One who has shone *in* our hearts to give the light of the knowledge of the glory of God in the face of Christ. (emphasis added)

These may be Paul's most provocative words regarding his own ministry. Paul is saying, "This is not about me. We do not advance ourselves." The word translated "preach" (*kērussrō*) carries with it the word picture of a herald. The herald was a first-century "verbal newspaper" who, after the victories of a king, would walk the streets dispensing the word, proclaiming that victory was assured by their leader, and thus giving the people great confidence. Obviously, this metaphor has powerful implications for the gospel preacher, who assures the world that their King is victorious. Paul is saying that our purpose is not to trumpet ourselves. We do not minister for the purpose of getting the word out about ourselves, our opinions, or our lives. So what does Paul mean that we do not preach ourselves?

The context, found in 3:15–16, is Paul's discussion of his

unbelieving Jewish brothers, who were perishing because "to this day whenever Moses is read, a veil lies over their heart; but whenever a person turns to the Lord, the veil is taken away." Paul then proceeds to make four profound statements.

First, *the unbeliever is completely in the dark.* Those who choose not to believe in Christ are actually blinded by Satan so that they cannot see anything. Later, Paul would refer to those without Christ as "dead in your trespasses and sins, in which you formerly walked according to the course of this world, according to the prince of the power of the air" (Eph. 2:1–2). Perhaps the most compelling evidence of this truth is anecdotal. The preacher is preaching with great passion the message of the gospel, yet it appears that those listening have no comprehension of what is being said. Their unbelief illustrates the fact that they are completely in the dark. They are. It is hard to believe that someone could actually reject the sweet message of Jesus. However, a blind man in the Louvre may be surrounded with the most precious works of art ever produced, but he feels nothing, for he sees nothing. He is in the dark. Jesus described this as seed on the road (Mark 4:1–20). Similarly, the unbeliever does not respond when the precious life of Christ is before him—he is in the dark.

Second, Paul says that only *Christ turns the light on.* "For God, who said, 'Light shall shine out of darkness,' is the One who has shone in our hearts to give the light of the knowledge of the glory of God in the face of Christ" (v. 6). This is an obvious allusion to creation: "God said, 'Let there be light,' and there was light" (Gen. 1:3). In the absolute nothingness that existed, God created light. All that previously existed was the abyss, darkness. Then God, who is the source of all light, infused something (light) into nothing (darkness). In the same way that God made light from nothing, He goes into the human heart, in the act of proclamation, and flips the switch. The metaphor makes it clear that the preacher is the *means* of God's ignition. The metaphor also makes it clear that the preacher is not the *source* of the ignition.

Preaching is a daunting task. We stand there before people in our imperfection. Our ambition is that God will save and sanctify, but even as we preach we are struggling with our own sanctification. And yet, out of this darkness flows the light, and into their darkness comes the light. Note that Paul does not say that God shines *on* the heart but *in* the heart. In the same way that God made something from nothing in creation, He causes light to be formed in the heart of the unbeliever. This is the internal reality of preaching. We preach the gospel, and the Spirit goes into the human heart and ignites it.

There is also an external reality—the light is flowing from God, through me, and on them.[2] Perhaps Paul is considering his own experience of being blinded by the light of Christ. From Paul's darkness, light flowed forth and is now illuminating the hearts of others. The metaphor can be seen from two perspectives. From the preacher's perspective, the light is flowing from God, through the preacher, and on to the people. From God's perspective, in the darkness of unbelief God ignites a spiritual fire that causes the heart to be illuminated with the glory of Christ. Now the question is, How does this take place?

Third, Paul says that Satan is trying to keep unbelievers from seeing *"the light of the gospel of the glory of Christ, who is the image of God."* The light is trying to penetrate, but it cannot because Satan has blinded the minds of the unbelieving. The light here is the light of the gospel. Paul did not have a completed canon of Scripture. However, it would not be unfair to the Pauline scheme to understand the gospel message as that which is proclaimed from Scripture—all of Scripture.

This makes sense since all of Scripture speaks of Christ. In response to the Jews' rejection of the testimony to Christ, He responded, "You search the Scriptures because you think that in them you have eternal life; it is these that testify of Me" (John 5:39). After the crucifixion and resurrection of Christ, He appeared to two disciples while they were walking on the road to Emmaus. Jesus pulled alongside of them and "beginning with Moses and with all the prophets, He explained to them the things concerning Himself in all the Scripture" (Luke 24:27). It is clear that in the mind of Christ, the Old Testament was

---

2. See Paul Barnett, *The Second Epistle to the Corinthians*, New International Commentary on the New Testament (Grand Rapids: Eerdmans, 1997), 224.

a testimony to the coming Christ. This was also clear to the apostle Paul. As the book of Acts comes to a close, Luke paints a picture of Paul, in his own quarters, receiving guests and "explaining to them by solemnly testifying about the kingdom of God and trying to persuade them concerning Jesus, from both the Law and the Prophets" (Acts 28:23b). It is obvious that the New Testament is about the coming of Christ and the way He manifested Himself in the life of the church. However, it seems clear that both in the mind of Christ and in the mind of Paul, the function of the Old Testament Scriptures was to bear witness to Christ as well.

One more Scripture is worth noting. As Paul was nearing the end of his ministry, he gave his closing admonition to his young protégé Timothy to "preach the word" (2 Tim. 4:2). While this text is often used to advocate being faithful to Scripture, it is fair to ask what the "word" was that Timothy was to preach, since Paul was not referring to the New Testament. Earlier, in 2 Timothy 3:15–17, Paul wrote,

> You, however, continue in the things you have learned and become convinced of, knowing from whom you have learned them, and that from childhood you have known the sacred writings which are able to give you the wisdom that leads to salvation through faith which is in Christ Jesus. All Scripture is inspired by God and profitable for teaching, for reproof, for correction, for training in righteousness; so that the man of God may be adequate, equipped for every good work.

This text is so often mined for pastoral instruction that the theological thrust of Paul's thought is sometimes missed. Look at verse 15 carefully. Paul is saying that the sacred writings, Timothy's Old Testament, were able to lead to salvation in Christ! So not only does the Old Testament allude to Christ, but it also has the power to lead someone to faith in Christ. So when Paul says to Timothy to preach the Word, he is saying, "Timothy, preach Jesus from the Old Testament." What a provocative thought. Christ is the sum and total of all that is in the sacred Scriptures. There are volumes more that could be said at this point; however, there should be no question that in the mind of Paul and in the mind of Christ, *the function of all Scripture was to point to Christ.*[3] This allows us to see the texts of Scripture as they stand in the whole of salvation history and provides a Christological center to our preaching, a center that is where preaching was intended to be. If this is already your conviction, you will forgive the diversion. However, all of this helps us frame a contextual backdrop for 2 Corinthians 4:4 and 6.

In the Greek, Paul piles up genitives here at the end of verse 6: "*of* the Glory of God . . . *of* Christ." Notice the progression. They cannot see God, because they cannot see Christ; they cannot see Christ because *their minds are blinded to the preached Word.* One cannot read Pauline literature as a whole and not embrace the truth that in verse 4, and later in verse 6, Paul is making an explicit claim that the glory of Christ *is* in the gospel message, which for us is the revealed Word of God, our Bible. Notice this enthralling concept. As the Word of God is preached, people stay in darkness if they do not hear the Word, because the Word speaks of Christ and Christ reveals the Father. This same progression is found at the end of verse 6: "For God, who said, 'Light shall shine out of darkness,'" is the One who has shone in our hearts to give the light of the knowledge of the glory of God in the face of Christ." Notice the progression again:

Verse 4	Verse 6
Light of the gospel	In our hearts
Of the glory	Of the knowledge
Of Christ	Of the glory of God
Who is the image of God	In the face of Christ

---

3. For further discussion of how this manifests itself in a sermon structure, see Bryan Chapell, *Christ-Centered Preaching* (Grand Rapids: Baker, 2005). For a discussion of how to preach Christ from the Old Testament, among many helpful works are Graeme Goldsworthy, *Preaching the Whole Bible as Christian Scripture* (Grand Rapids: Eerdmans, 2000); and Sidney Greidnaus, *Preaching Christ from the Old Testament* (Grand Rapids: Eerdmans, 1999).

If we were to rephrase these verses in a chronological sequence, it would go like this:

1. God communicates Himself through Christ.
2. Christ is the perfect reflection of the Father.
3. The gospel message is the "gospel of Christ."
4. Therefore, the gospel in our hearts brings us to Christ, who then brings us to the Father.

From God's perspective we could diagram it like this:

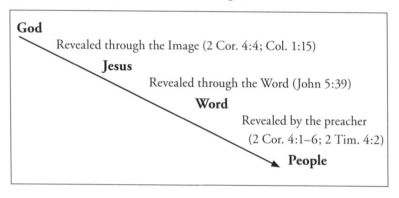

The idea is that God is revealed in Christ, Christ is revealed in the Word, and the Word is revealed by the preacher. In this way, the preacher stands in God's direct revelation of Himself. God shines in our hearts for the purpose of giving others the knowledge of the gospel of Christ.

In a later moment of self-description, Paul confesses that "for this reason I found mercy, so that in me as the foremost, Jesus Christ might demonstrate His perfect patience as an example for those who would believe in Him for eternal life" (1 Tim. 1:16). God had shown mercy to this world-class sinner and hater of God, so that all other sinners could look at him and say, "There must be hope for me!" The word "example" (*hupotupōsis*) in the above text describes the artist's sketch that he uses as a first draft and by which he patterns the rest of the painting. Paul is saying, "God saved me for one reason. I have been shown mercy so that unbelievers can stand and gawk, thinking that the God who did it for Paul could surely do it for them." Preachers are not the sun, the source of light. We are the moon. We reflect a light whose source is Christ. Our hearts have been illumined for the purpose of being used by God in the process of illumination for those who do not believe. How does God, in harmony with man's free will, reach into darkness and flip the spiritual switch so that the unbeliever can see? What is the divine means of illumination?

Fourth, Paul concludes that *it is necessary that the preacher not preach himself but Christ only*. The unbeliever is in the dark; Christ turns the light on, and *proclamation* is used by God in the process of illumination. Therefore, the damnable sin of the preacher is to put anything before people less than the message of Christ, the Word. If textual intricacies are the focus of preaching, if practical insights are the focus of preaching, if cultural events are the focus of preaching, then we have not put before people the only thing that can cause them to see: Jesus. He is the Light. Again, we are walking though the Louvre with blind people, wondering why they are not moved. We are at a concert with deaf people, wondering why they do not get it. If the text is not center, then Christ is not the focus. If Christ is not the focus of preaching, they will not—they cannot—see Him. Only Christ can turn the light on. Our purpose is not to entertain or project how good we are. Our objective is to be a clear conduit for the light. And that clarity demands that we die for the people so that they can see the light through us and we do not become an impediment to the light.

It is not too unusual to hear from my students before the first day of preaching class, but I did not expect this e-mail. A student wrote to say that he was born with a speech impediment. He was enrolled in my preaching class where performance was a major part of the grade. He could do it, he said, he just wanted to let me know that he had a speech impediment, which would limit his performance. And I do too. Not the kind that he had. But all of our preaching is impeded by the very fact that it is we who are preaching. My impediment is, well, myself. If I do not check myself, the medium of communication can impede the content of what is being preached, limiting its effectiveness.

Preaching is such a powerful art that, if left alone, the medium of preaching becomes its message. Paul is suggesting a horrific, criminal irony: the means of preaching displaces the message of preaching. The preacher, not Christ, becomes the focus of the preaching. The net effect of this switch is that the light is not turned on. One cannot see the stars very well in the city. A few small watts of artificial city light are all it takes to hide the authentic, blazing light of the heavenly luminaries. Preaching ourselves, even in small, inconsequential ways, can be the few small lumens that keep people from the true, satisfying, glorious light of Christ. And, if we are standing in the artificial light of self-service, we will never see the glory of Christ or be able to reflect His light. Consequently, those without the light of the Word do not see the glory of the light of Christ and therefore do not see God. This is what it means to "preach ourselves."

How do I know if I am preaching myself? The ways to preach oneself are many; so it is a little dangerous to make a list, since it might suggest that if our particular temptation is not on the list, then we are fine. But this is not exhaustive; it is designed to provoke thought. We might be preaching ourselves if . . .

1. Our sermons are filled with personal illustrations designed to draw attention to ourselves, more than to the text.
2. We use illustrations that do not illustrate the text and therefore draw attention away from it.
3. We do not pay the price to study but defer to our own interest.
4. We do not explain the text carefully but choose to advance our opinion on a text. This is exalting our wisdom above God's agenda.
5. We use a sermon structure that is predetermined instead of letting the structure of the text become the structure of the sermon.

6. We decide before studying the text that we will follow a rhetorical pattern, an emotional vibe or feel, instead of letting the emotion of the text drive the sermon.
7. We do not understand the text deeply before we preach it.
8. We decide that our desire not to have any attention drawn to us is more important than the people understanding the text. Therefore we never take any risk in the pulpit and defer to our covert pride that is masked as shyness.
9. We decide that drawing attention to self is more important than drawing attention to the text.

The problem with all of the above is that the text points to Christ. So any time we are preaching ourselves, we are not preaching the text and therefore not preaching Christ. To put a fine point on it, to preach myself is to displace focus on Christ with focus on me. Without the text, our listeners do not know Christ; without Christ, they do not know God. Preaching ourselves is the most effective way to create Pharisees, people who are always there in the congregation but are never brought to face the text.

CONCLUSION

We have to embrace the reality that the act of preaching is itself a message so powerful that if we preachers are not vigilant, it will become the message and not the means to the message. If the medium of preaching becomes the message of preaching, and we are the catalysts for the medium, then we are in essence preaching about ourselves. And this takes us back to our first question.

In summary, this is the first question, and it is a theological one: How has God revealed Himself? The answer is through Jesus, and Jesus is revealed in the Word. Now we are ready to answer the second question: What method best accomplishes the goal of revealing the text and therefore revealing Christ, who will reveal the Father? I would submit that only a message that is driven by the substance, structure, and spirit of a biblical text will, over time, lead people to see Christ in His Word and, as a result, see the Father in Christ. This could be an expository sermon, inasmuch as *expository* is understood as text-driven preaching. The last question—the very last question—is a question of delivery style: What about my personality and context shapes this presentation? I understand that if we never ask the delivery question, we risk becoming boring exegetes, mindlessly walking through the text without ever truly communicating. However, there is a greater risk in asking the last question first. If style trumps all, we become stylized showmen engaging the senses and not the Word. And remember—please get this—if in our sermons our hearers do not get the meaning of the text, they do not get Christ, and if they do not get Christ, they do not get the Father. This is His chosen means of communication. I have neither the liberty nor the license to make preaching anything less.

God didn't give me a vote or ask for my opinion on this. Preaching is not invention; it is proclamation. Preaching is preaching the Word, for the very reason that the Word is always revealing Christ, and Christ is always revealing the Father.

From here we can move to the most explicit passage on dying in ministry so that others may live. It is found in Colossians 1:24, where we are called to invite people to join Christ by means of our extending the sufferings of Christ to them. Warning: this passage is not for the faint of heart.

[4]

Invite

Sharing the Sufferings of Christ

A preacher must extend the sufferings of Christ to others so they may be invited to acknowledge the Center of all things as the center of their lives.

Now I rejoice in my sufferings for your sake, and in my flesh I do my share on behalf of His body, which is the church, in filling up what is lacking in Christ's afflictions.
—Colossians 1:24

Perhaps Colossians 1:24 isn't the most confusing verse of Paul's. But it's close. How could this beleaguered apostle suggest that there was something deficient in the suffering of Christ? And, furthermore, how could he suggest that he could fill in what was missing? Hasn't he read—well—Paul? For example, in Romans Paul wrote,

Being justified as a gift by His grace through the redemption which is in Christ Jesus; whom God displayed publicly as a propitiation in His blood through faith. This was to demonstrate His righteousness, because in the forbearance of God He passed over the sins previously committed; for the demonstration, I say, of His righteousness at the present time, so that He would be just and the justifier of the one who has faith in Jesus. (3:23–26)

Much more then, having been justified by His blood, we
shall be saved from the wrath of God through Him. (5:9)

Through one act of righteousness there resulted justification
of life to all men . . . so through the obedience of the One the
many will be made righteous. (5:18b, 19b)

More immediately, in Colossians itself Paul wrote that

when you were dead in your transgressions and the uncir-
cumcision of your flesh, He made you alive together with
Him, having forgiven us all our transgressions, having can-
celed out the certificate of debt consisting of decrees against
us, which was hostile to us; and He has taken it out of the
way, having nailed it to the cross. (2:13–14)

It's clear enough that Paul identified Christ *alone* as the means of
reconciliation with the Father. He writes, "He has now reconciled you
in His fleshly body through death" (Col. 1:22). Paul understood that
Christ—and Christ only—can forgive sins. It also seems clear that
Paul thought that Christ's death was enough to forgive all sins. So
if His death was enough, why would Paul suggest that he could fill
"what is lacking in Christ's afflictions" (v. 24)?

Colossians 1:24 is so important that perhaps it is impossible to understand the idea of suffering in ministry without a firm grasp on its
meaning. So, what does it mean?

In the next pages, we will try to unpack its meaning and apply it
specifically to preaching.

EXPOSITION OF COLOSSIANS 1:24

Context

The verses leading up to Colossians 1:24 feature the motif of progression and growth. Look at it throughout the chapter:

- 1:5: You previously heard the word.
- 1:9–10: We have prayed that you "will walk in a manner worthy of the Lord."
- 1:12: God has "qualified us to share in the inheritance of the saints in Light."

The mention of the light leads Paul to present a most scintillating Christology in verses 13–20. From this Christological climax, he reinforces the idea of progression in verses 21–23:

> And although you were formerly alienated and hostile in mind, engaged in evil deeds, yet He has now reconciled you in His fleshly body through death, in order to present you before Him holy and blameless and beyond reproach—if indeed you continue in the faith firmly established and steadfast, and not moved away from the hope of the gospel that you have heard, which was proclaimed in all creation under heaven, and of which I, Paul, was made a minister.

While the church in Colossae was challenged with a unique heretical drift, Paul is generally thrilled at their spiritual *progress*. Imagine receiving an e-mail from a church where you had previously ministered and learning that the gospel had worked mightily. The people were saved, and they were progressing in sanctification. Things were right. You would be ecstatic. This is how Paul felt. And like a proud father swelling with pride over their spiritual well-being, Paul explains *his* part in all this. Interestingly, Paul does not use the parent motif of 1 Thessalonians 2. Paul's own understanding of his role in their salvation in sanctification is surprising.

Now I Rejoice in My Sufferings

Paul first rejoices that he is able to suffer for the Colossians' sake. What suffering? Well, Paul is writing from a Roman prison (Col. 4:18; Acts 28:16–31). It seems that Paul assumes the readers are familiar with his situation since he does not feel compelled to mention it specifically in this verse.

We can imagine the apostle sitting in darkness, shackles around his ankles. And, unlike a dictating scribe, he is writing this with his own hand (Col. 4:18). Maybe even the physical act of writing is painful. So while he is excited with their progress in the gospel, he cannot discuss their progress without mentioning his own suffering.

This is a typical theme in Paul—he finds joy in suffering. And it is a Christian ideal: rejoice in trials (Rom. 5:3; James 1:2), consider yourself blessed to be able to suffer for Christ (Acts 5:41), because present suffering cannot compare with future glory (Rom. 8:18). Ultimately, Paul understood himself as "crucified with Christ" (Gal. 2:20). The idea is that of joy and gladness, which for Paul always "is bound up with his work as an apostle."[1] So the gladness that he experienced was a fruit of the people he served.

However, there is something else going on here. He is not just glad about the people; he is glad about one particular truth. The reason is not that he is infused with grace accessible only to super-apostles; rather, his joy is in the knowledge of something very specific. Paul is overjoyed that his sufferings are "filling up what is lacking in Christ's afflictions."

Filling Up What Is Lacking in Christ's Afflictions

There is no way to explain away this unsettling verse using the Greek language. It is unambiguous.[2] The sense is that the sufferings

---

1. Gerhard Kittel, Geoffrey William Bromiley, and Gerhard Friedrich, *Theological Dictionary of the New Testament*, electronic ed. (Grand Rapids: Eerdmans, 1964–1976), S. 9:369.

2. What is ambiguous to some is whether Paul is suffering to fill up what is lacking in the sufferings of Christ, or if he is filling up what is lacking in the sufferings of the body of Christ, the church. I am writing from the position that the genitive τοῦ χριστοῦ is a reference to the afflictions of Christ that He suffered on earth, specifically His death, and not a reference to the sufferings of the body of Christ. This seems to be more consistent with 2 Corinthians 4:10, where Paul is "always carrying about in the body the dying of Jesus, so that the life of Jesus also may be manifested in our body."

For a discussion of this tension, see R. McL. Wilson, *A Critical and Exegetical Commentary on Colossians and Philemon*, International Critical Commentary on the Holy Scriptures of the Old and New Testaments (London: T & T Clark, 2005), 168–72. Also see the following:

of Christ, which he experienced in His atoning death and sinless life, were missing something. The sufferings of Christ were incomplete according to Paul.

As noted, there is no way someone could honestly read Paul and conclude that he believed Christ's suffering was insufficient. What Christ did was completely sufficient. And yet, His affliction created a vacuum. It is in one way insufficient: it is in one way short, lacking. Stunted. In one way the suffering Christ is not enough. It needs something added to it. Yet, how could this be?

Christ's sacrifice was stunted in that for His sacrifice to continue to affect the Colossians' spiritual progress, Paul would have to suffer for them as well. Not in an atoning way, but in a real way nonetheless, Paul must extend the sufferings from Calvary to Colossae.[3] In other words, Paul was suffering in a way that Christ would have suffered had He been there. Paul's suffering does not save them, but it is an extension of the suffering of Christ. In this way Paul was filling up what was lacking in Christ's afflictions. He was suffering in the stead of Christ to further affect their spiritual progress.

While this can be a difficult passage to understand, the idea that the believer must suffer in Christ is supported by the following passages.[4]

If they called the master of the house Beelzebub, how much more them of his household. (Matt. 10:25)

You shall be hated of all men for my name's sake. (Mark 13:13)

Handley C. G. Moule, *Colossians and Philemon* (Westwood, NJ: Revell, n.d.), 99–100; E. F. Scott, *The Epistles of Paul to the Colossians, to Philemon and to the Ephesians*, Moffat New Testament Commentary (London: Hodder and Stoughton, 1930), 28–31; and Peter T. O'Brien, *Colossians, Philemon*, Word Biblical Commentary (Waco, TX: Word, 1982), 75–83.

3. For a discussion of this tension, see Wilson, *A Critical and Exegetical Commentary on Colossians and Philemon*, 168–72. Also see the following: Moule, *Colossians and Philemon*, 99–100; Scott, *Epistles of Paul to the Colossians, to Philemon and to the Ephesians*, 28–31; and O'Brien, *Colossians, Philemon*, 75–83.

4. William Hendrickson. *Philippians, Colossians, Philemon*, New Testament Commentary (Grand Rapids: Baker, 1979), 87. Translation is Hendrickson's.

If the world hates you, know that it has hated me before it hated you. . . . But all these things will they do to you for my name's sake, because they do not know the One who sent me. (John 15:18–21)

Saul, Saul, why do you persecute me? . . . I am, whom you are persecuting. (Acts 9:4–5)

The afflictions of Christ overflow toward us. (2 Cor. 1:5)

. . . always bearing about in the body the putting to death of Jesus. (2 Cor. 4:10)

I bear on my body the marks of Jesus. (Gal. 6:17)

. . . that I may know him . . . and the fellowship of his sufferings. (Phil. 3:10)

Of course we do not participate in the atonement of Christ. That is His work alone. However, in these limited ways we share in the suffering of Christ.

What Jesus Will Not Do

To say that Christ was still suffering for the Colossians would have been wrong. He suffered once for all (Heb. 7:27; 9:12, 26, 28; 10:10). Christ has atoned for sins and is presently at the right hand of God. Christ, the sacrificial Lamb of God, now functions as a mediator between God and man. He is at the right hand of God, mediating for us.

In order to accomplish this goal of mediation, to allow the work of the Holy Spirit to carry out Christ's promise, Christ must necessarily be at the right hand of the Father. Therefore, Jesus was not going to walk from Jerusalem to Colossae. No, Paul would have to do that, suffering in Christ's suffering and for Christ's body. He would have to extend the suffering from Jerusalem to Colossae for the very reason that Christ was not crucified in Colossae but in Jerusalem. Christ was not going to sit in a cold prison and write an encouraging letter, Jesus was not going to stand in front of the Sanhedrin, Jesus was not there to be shipwrecked on Malta. Paul would have to do all those things. Paul would have to extend the sufferings of Christ in that way.

Neither will Jesus stand with trembling knees in front of God's sheep with a Bible in His hand and preach. You will have to do that. You will have to extend the suffering of the pulpit from Jerusalem to your town. Jesus will not. His sacrifices have stopped there. He will not physically sacrifice to know the people, to communicate to the people, and to study the Word. He is receiving His reward. And to receive our reward, we must extend the sufferings of Christ in ministry, and specifically in the act of preaching.[5] Christ has suffered; now you must suffer, so that the suffering experienced by Christ may be known to those who do not know. This is doing our share.

Filling Up

By dying so they might live, Paul "fills up" (*antanaplaro*) what is lacking in the sufferings of Christ. The root of this word is also found in verse 19 of the same chapter, where Paul notes that Christ is the fullness (*plaroma*) of God. There seems to be a distant, yet important, relationship between the two concepts.

In verse 19 Paul is saying that all that God wanted to reveal of Himself was expressed in the person of Christ. Classic Gnosticism as we understand it was not in full bloom at this point in history, but the Colossians were given to a specific heresy. The heresy suggested that while Christ was indeed a divine expression, there were other emanations or spirits who, along with Christ, were worthy of worship.

---

5. Note in this regard 1 Timothy 4:16: "Pay close attention to yourself and to your teaching; persevere in these things, for as you do this you will ensure salvation both for yourself and for those who hear you"; and 1 Corinthians 3:12–15: "Now if any man builds on the foundation with gold, silver, precious stones, wood, hay, straw, each man's work will become evident; for the day will show it because it is *to be* revealed with fire, and the fire itself will test the quality of each man's work. If any man's work which he has built on it remains, he will receive a reward. If any man's work is burned up, he will suffer loss; but he himself will be saved, yet so as through fire."

So perhaps in a chilling rhetorical strike, Paul is saying that all that needs to be worshipped is Christ. He is the fullness of God—all this is needed to understand and access deity.

I do not intend to suggest a closer relationship between verses 19 and 24 than actually exists. However, if Paul is to fill up the sufferings of Christ, this indeed is a very Christological idea. God wanted to communicate Himself, and so Christ suffered to fully express God (Heb. 1:2). For the eternal Word to be incarnate, He would have to take on the chains of a man, the prison of a body (Phil. 2:5–11; John 1:1–5). All of this suffering was necessary so that He could communicate God to the world. This He could communicate because He was the fullness. And yet, five verses later, Paul says that He was filling up the sufferings of this Fullness. So in order for Christ to be obedient, He had to suffer to express the fullness of God. For Paul to be obedient, he had to fill up the sufferings of Christ. This was obedience for Christ, and it was sanctification for Paul.

Now if it is the desire for Christ to make us into His image (Rom. 8:29), and this includes those who proclaim the Word, then to be made into the image of Christ means that, like Christ, each preacher must suffer to fill up the afflictions to others, and in this way imitate Christ in His suffering to be the fullness of God. Christ suffered to make the atonement effective. We suffer to make the atonement known.

I Do My Share

We excluded an important phrase in the verse, and we will return to it now. Paul writes, "I do my share on behalf of His body." Paul is suggesting that the suffering that he is doing, he is doing corporately on behalf of the church. By this statement he asserts that his suffering for the body alone is not enough. This is interesting in light of verse 18, where Paul observed that due to Christ's resurrection and implied suffering, he won the right to be the head of the church. For this body Paul also is suffering, but he is not suffering alone. He is not doing all of it; he is doing some. Christ's suffering was enough to effect the whole of salvation. But Paul's suffering for the advance of the gospel is quite incomplete outside of other suffering done for the body of Christ. So if Paul is doing *his share* in filling up what is lacking, and his share was only a part, then there is *still lack* in the sufferings of Christ.

My friend Davy is taking the gospel to a closed country in Asia because he is filling up what is lacking in the sufferings of Christ. When I read this verse, I think of Ron, Brian, Greg, Elijah, Korvan, and a dozen other friends who are with Christ in the hard places around the world. They are there because, while Christ's atonement is enough, the people just do not know it. These servants of Christ are not filling up something that Christ did not do. They are suffering for the very reason that Christ is enough, but people do not know it. There is suffering to secure salvation—what Christ did. And there is also suffering for people to hear about salvation—what we do. The people in that Asian country were not at Calvary, so Davy is bringing Calvary to them.

This is exactly the point. What was missing for the Colossians, Paul filled. And by doing his share, he fully carried out the gospel (v. 25). So, Paul's partial participation in filling up Christ's afflictions was the full measure of his ministry. Likewise, when you are called upon to declare the Word of God, you look at a people who have access to the full atoning work of Christ, but the atonement is lacking inasmuch as they do not understand it. So you fill it up. You extend the sufferings of Christ to them so that they can hear the message. Remember, it's not about potency; it's about proximity. The gospel will save anyone anytime, anywhere, but it will not propagate itself. It moves only as those who move it move.[6]

The Centrality of Christ

In Colossians 1:15–20 Paul argues that Christ is supreme over all things. He argues Christ's supremacy with four proofs:

---

6. See E. M. Bounds, *Power Through Prayer* (Springdale, PA: Whitaker House, 1982), 11.

1. Christ is supreme because He is the perfect reflection of God (vv. 15a, 19).
2. Christ is supreme over all because of His relationship to creation (vv. 15b–17).
3. Christ is supreme over the church because by His resurrection, He won the right to be head of the church (v. 18).
4. Christ is supreme over all things because of His reconciliation of the world to Himself (v. 20).

The point is clear: Christ is everything because He alone is unique. Christ is not the highest priority, nor is He the first among others. He stands alone as the center of everything. He is awarded this place by His Father who, because of Christ's sacrifice, is completely committed to Christ's exaltation.

When a fourteenth-century mathematician and astronomer asserted that the sun was the center of our solar system, he was mocked. The sun could not be the center, the critics argued, the earth must be the center for we were created in God's image. And yet, all the critics of Copernicus did not alter the position of the sun one degree. They simply had to adjust their lives according to a reality that they could not control.

Living in the light of Christ's supremacy does not mean that we "make Him Lord"; we cannot make Him anything, much less what He already says that He is. No, we simply acknowledge that God, committed to the exaltation of His obedient Son, has chosen to allow Christ to reign forever as the center of all things. My right, privilege, and only response to this reality is to adjust my life according to what God already has established as true.

This is why it is terribly fascinating that at the close of this chapter, Paul makes the following assertions:

1. Paul's suffering is fully carrying out the preaching of the Word (v. 25).
2. The word he is preaching is a mystery (v. 26).

3. The mystery is Christ in you (v. 27).
4. The goal of his preaching is completeness in Christ (v. 28).
5. This is the whole reason Paul suffers (v. 29).

It would seem that this is a fascinating, doctrinally rich, impractical section of Scripture, until you see how Paul closes the chapter. He says in verse 27 that the mystery is Christ in you. This is indeed a mystery. After explaining that Christ is supreme over all things, he asserts the mind-blowing reality that the Christ who administrates all of heaven, who is the source of all that is good, who is the head of the church, who is the infrastructure that holds all the substance of this world together, desires to live in you! Could there be anything more fascinating? How could the One whose very essence is life be in my life? How could the Creator come to live in the creation? Could there be greater condescension? Could there be more humility? There is no other truth that I know that should throw us to our knees in grateful submission more than the glad and heavy truth that the One who is central to everything desires to be in me. So as I acknowledge His centrality, He graciously centers my life. This—and this alone—is the hope of our eternal life. If Christ is in me, then the glory that is within me will carry me into eternal glory when this corpse is buried.

The point is—and please read this carefully—*this is why we are suffering.* Extending the sufferings of Christ is not the romantic stuff of quasi Green Beret preachers who want to go to the next level. It *is* preaching. It *is* ministry. Ministry is nothing if it is not presenting "every man complete in Christ" (Col. 1:28). Therefore, we must identify the center of everything, which is Christ, and realize that most of the world is off center. People are floating out in the stratosphere of their own joys, their own pleasures, or their own misguided notions of truth, happily allowing lower luminaries to eclipse His magnificence. And yet, even if they believe this with perfect integrity, it does not matter what star, planet, or moon they call the center; only Christ is the center. The gravitational pull of the flesh, the world's system, and the Devil himself are so strong that it is impossible for someone to come to the center, unless someone else takes them there. And that intergalactic journey, bringing one from the margins to the center, requires suffering. It requires death. This is where it is analogous to preaching:

Paul suffered for the church.	We suffer in preaching Christ.
Paul filled up Christ's afflictions.	Suffering in preaching is an extension of the sufferings of Christ.
Paul suffered to present people complete in Christ.	We preach so that people will acknowledge the centrality of Christ and be complete.

APPLICATION: SO WHAT DOES THIS HAVE TO DO WITH PREACHING?

If I could switch metaphors, imagine a battlefield. But this battlefield is unique. The only safe zone is in the middle. Anyone who gets to the middle is safe, and your one job is to get people safely in the center. But the problem is, if you go out to capture some to bring them back to the center, you might die. Thus, if you want to bring people back, you cannot be afraid to die. Those consumed with their own safety will never bring people back to center. To say it another way, the reason people out in the field are dying is because so few are willing to die for them. The more those in the center think of their own safety, the more they lose ground and the more people die.

Death is in the pew because few are willing to die in the pulpit. Preaching is fearlessly going out among the Enemy and bringing people back to the center, for when they are in the center, the Center is in them, and they are safe. They are so safe that they too can risk going out and bringing others to the center.

[5]

Identify

Bearing the Reproach of Christ

Bearing the reproach of Christ allows us to
identify with the gospel we propagate.

*For the bodies of those animals whose blood is brought
into the holy place by the high priest as an offering for sin,
are burned outside the camp. Therefore Jesus also, that
He might sanctify the people through His own blood, suffered outside the gate. So, let us go out to Him outside the
camp, bearing His reproach. For here we do not have a lasting city, but we are seeking the city which is to come.*

—Hebrews 13:11–14

Let me ask a question: How do you manage your self-perception as
a preacher? When you think about yourself as a preacher or pastor, what do you think about? Do you perceive of yourself as a business leader, carefully navigating the challenges of a well-planned day?
Do you perceive of yourself as a chaplain, watching patiently over
the sick and affirmed and providing comfort where needed? Do you
perceive of yourself as the catalyst, the hub of the ministry, without
which things would fall apart?

I hate to admit this, but I've found myself at times using ministry
as a means of managing who I think I am, instead of understanding

who God already declared me to be. Consequently, decision making was about managing the perception of others, not doing what was best for a given situation. This is why this next text is so helpful. It clarifies our identity as Christians, and consequently as preachers. True, there is indeed something unique about Christian ministry. However, what is true of all Christians is at least true of preachers. So let's take a look at another daunting text and consider its implications for preaching.

EXPOSITION OF HEBREWS 13:15

Context

The Jewish believers who received the letter to the Hebrews were struggling. Apparently they had not yet made up their mind whether to follow Christ or to retain the Judaism of their fathers. They were not completely convinced that Christ was the center of everything, so they still struggled with clinging to the bright yet marginal luminary of the Jewish faith and calling it the center of everything. But there cannot be two centers. They could either claim that Christ was the center of all things or Judaism was the center, but not both. So, in an effort to move them closer to the center, the author encourages them to see the parallels between Judaism and Christianity. He then shows them that Jesus Christ is "the author and finisher of our faith" (12:2 NKJV). Christ actually is the culmination of the Jewish faith; they simply could not see it.

As he concludes, the author offers a practical word. Specifically, he wants his readers to be free from the legalism of the old dietary laws. But in an interesting parallel between dietary laws and Christ, he says, "We have an altar from which those who serve the tabernacle have no right to eat" (13:10). The altar he is referring to is Christ. This table is not reserved for priests, but for all who will come to Christ.

Outside the Camp

Then the writer draws an amazing parallel. He observes that the animals that were sacrificed were then burned outside the camp. This is a reference to the priestly practice during the Day of Atonement. After the blood of an animal was poured out in sacrifice, the remaining flesh of the animal was taken outside the camp to be burned. It seems that this was not only hygienic but symbolic. The animal represented sin, and no one should be associated with the sin. In fact, the one who took the animal out of the camp was commanded to bathe and change clothes before coming back into the camp (Lev. 16:27–28).

In the same way that the animals were burned outside the camp, Christ was crucified outside the city. According to John 19:17, Jesus was taken to Golgotha, which was outside the city gates of Jerusalem. What a filthy parallel. The animal representing sin, whose flesh was to be burned, is analogous to our sweet Savior, who died for us. Here is the difference: the one who carried the body of the animal was commanded to disassociate himself from the animal quickly; we are commanded to go out and identify with Christ, "bearing His reproach" (Heb. 13:13). To the Jewish mind, this is a hellacious metaphor. There is no question that in this gutsy parallel, the author is calling his readers to a vicious obedience. Who in their right mind would actually go out and associate with the dead, lifeless corpse of the animal? Who would associate with the animal so unfortunate as to be killed for the sins of the Israelites? But the metaphor works. Here's why. While Christ was brutally murdered, He gave His life willingly. He was not led to the cross against His will. No one took His life from Him. Rather, He laid it down willingly that He might sanctify us (v. 12). The result of the crucifixion was that we were set apart on a journey to be shaped into Christlikeness (Rom. 8:28–30).

When an animal died, it was just a poor, hapless animal; the rank victim of demanded justice. However, when Christ died, not only did the result of the sacrifice have value, but the Sacrifice Himself also had value. So in this case, if we understand and value the Sacrifice, we are perfectly willing to identify ourselves with the sacrifice. We are willing to "go outside the camp" and bear the reproach of Calvary—to be seen at the foot of the cross.

Identity

This idea of reproach bearing is interesting. Before we can apply this to preaching, we have to figure out what it means. The "reproach" of Hebrews 13:13 is identification with the dead sacrifice. However, the author is taking it one step further than identification; he is assuming that we also bear, hold, possess, or take on the sufferings of Christ. Identifying with the corpse of the dead sacrifice was to "bear" or take on the same shame the sacrifice took on. Perhaps the Revised Standard Version says it best: "bear the abuse he endured."

This is difficult now, and it was difficult then. None of the apostles, with the exception of John, went out to identify with Him. Rather, they hid themselves. Simon of Cyrene perhaps best epitomizes the idea. As an innocent bystander, he was forced to bear the cross of Christ and carry it up to Golgotha (Luke 23:26).

Jesus was maligned, hated, abused, mistrusted, heckled, jeered at, mocked, and misunderstood. He was blamed for inciting the crowds against the establishment, until the establishment killed Him. He was loved by the common people and then rejected by them. He was rejected by the religious establishment and killed by them. He gave His life for truth, and He gave His life for people. So to get up and go stand there at the cross is to incite all of this against you. Eventually people think the same things about you that they thought about Jesus. And this is the issue: *identity*. Simply put, we are to figure out where Christ is, leave the world's system of doing things, and go identify with Him—all for the simple reason that this is our identity. For the Jews who were reading Hebrews, the idea was clear. They had to go out from the old system of the Levitical code and bear the reproach and shame of being with Christ.

What is the application for us preachers? There is no physical cross we can go out to. However, Jesus is still outside the gate. He is still perceived as a hapless victim, and His message is as unpopular as it ever was. Perhaps "going outside the camp" has less to do with a physical place than with a mental state. In other words, as a preacher do I perceive of myself as one who identifies with Christ against the moral and religious climate, or do I try to explain my existence within it, without going outside the camp? Do I think of myself as

- an iconoclastic vision of counterculture?
- an entertainer whose pulpit is his showcase?
- everybody's friend, who is going to "like" people to Christ?
- a culture warrior armed and ready against all foes?
- a captain who is moving the kingdom forward?

I am not taking shots at others. There is a measure of identification in all of these. But God help us when we preachers spend our lives trying to identify ourselves with certain aspects of our culture, or certain aspects of our church culture, when our true identity is all wrapped up in the embarrassing, thirty-three-year-old Jew who hung naked between two thieves. That's who I am. That's who you are. That's our identity. With Christ, we go outside the camp. Where exactly is that? It is where the people are. The number one criticism of Christ was that He was a "friend of sinners." So to bear the reproach of Christ is to bear the reproach of association with those whom Christ loved. In sum, going outside the camp when we preach is preaching in a way that identifies us with Christ—we preach Christ from the Bible. Second, it is identifying with those whom Christ loved—we preach to sinners. Thus we are identifying with Christ by identifying with others.

Two Ways to Bear the Reproach in the Pulpit

Preaching Jesus

In John 5:39 Jesus said that the Old Testament Scriptures speak of Him. The statement actually was made to Jewish leaders who knew the Scripture quite well. He was telling them that the Old Testament they were using as a theological whipping stick to keep people in bondage was actually the written revelation of Christ Himself. Christ understood that He was the entire point of the Old Testament; so

when He had time to explain the Old Testament to His disciples, He
taught them how the Old Testament pointed to Him.

The scene takes place on the road to Emmaus after Christ's resurrection. The risen Lord comes alongside some followers who are
so engorged with despair they cannot see that Jesus takes up beside
them. Luke records that after they explain why they are discouraged,
Christ says to them,

> O foolish men and slow of heart to believe in all that the
> prophets have spoken! Was it not necessary for the Christ to
> suffer these things and to enter into His glory? Then begin-
> ning with Moses and with all the prophets, He explained
> to them the things concerning Himself *in all the Scriptures*.
> (Luke 24:25–27, emphasis added)

It is a little more than obvious that the New Testament is about
Christ. However, Christ understood that the witness of the Old Testament was a revelation of Himself as well. Therefore, there is not a
text that one can preach that will not ultimately point to Christ. The
point is not that every text is about Jesus as a person. Rather, the point
is that every text fits somewhere in the history of salvation. And, the
point of the history of salvation ultimately is to exalt Christ.

It seems clear, then, that when we open any text of the Bible, we
need to see how the text fits ultimately into salvation history. I am not
suggesting the predictability of ending each sermon the same way.
Rather, I am raising a pastoral concern. Should not our people, exposed to thousands of sermons, be able to connect the dots and see
how the Old Testament ultimately is fulfilled in Christ?

Paul's frequently quoted admonition to young Timothy to "preach
the word" (2 Tim. 4:2) is often understood as Paul's commendation
of expository preaching. However, since Timothy did not have the
New Testament, as we understand it, but did have the gospel witness,
it seems more precise to say that Paul was telling Timothy to preach
the Old Testament in light of the gospel.

So we have thirty minutes with half-engaged believers whose only curiosity is whether we can say something they have not heard before. The temptation is to find shelter under the perception that we are actually very attuned to popular culture or the world of politics, that we know "exactly how they feel," or that they believe their preacher is just "a great guy." There is nothing wrong with identifying with people— we must do this. And yet, we must make sure that we do not allow identification to subtly keep us from bearing the reproach of Christ. At the end of the sermon, we better be sure that we have borne the reproach of the cross, that with exegetical honesty we have so extracted Christ from the text that people are forced to decide if they also will go out and bear His reproach.

Preaching Jesus to People

Perhaps there is another extreme. This is where we identify the gospel message from a text but do not identify with the audience at all. The preacher goes through the motions of a sermon like a homiletic automaton—same style, same way, every week, no matter how the congregation has changed or is changing. Since this is the subject of chapter 7, it is enough here to simply say that boring sermons are not Christian. Sermons that do not go out to the cross and bear the reproach of Christ to love the ones He loved are not Christian. The New Testament was written in street language. When we muddy it up with unclear language, we miss the entire point of Scripture, because Christ died so people might hear the good news clearly; because they cannot believe unless they hear, and they cannot hear unless they have a preacher; and because the good news is good news only if it is understood. Those so tethered to one homiletic vision of a sermon will find themselves imposing that vision on any given text regardless of the audience or the genre.

This is not the way of Jesus. Jesus preached clearly so that we could understand clearly. Then the Holy Spirit of Jesus Christ inspired a canon of stories, letters, laws, poetry, history, and seemingly wild apocalyptic visions that are remarkable in their personal warmth and in their unmistakable identification with others. To identify with the reproach of Christ is to identify with those whom He loved. Perhaps the hardest prayer to pray is, "God keep me so laced to the text that I show them Christ exactly from the Scripture and so free from a desire to be identified with anything else that I communicate Christ alone." Christ is our identity. This is the challenge of bearing His reproach in the pulpit.

Enduring City

If this is so challenging, then why do it? Why fight to be identified with Christ alone? The reason we do so is mentioned in Hebrews 13:14: "For here we do not have a lasting city, but we are seeking the city which is to come." The idea of looking forward to a better place is a huge theme in the book of Hebrews. In chapter 11, the author lists those who have distinguished themselves as people of faith, noting their incredible sacrifices. Early in the chapter he notes Abraham and how he left all to follow the promise. Then in verses 13–16 he writes,

> These all died in faith, not having received the promise, but having seen them afar off were assured of them, embraced them and confessed that they were *strangers and pilgrims on the earth*. For those who say such things declare plainly that they seek a homeland. And truly if they had called to mind that country from which they had come out, they would have opportunity to return. But now they *desire a better, that is, a heavenly country*. Therefore God is not ashamed to be called their God, for He has *prepared a city* for them. (NKJV, emphasis added)

Do you see the progression? They understood that they were strangers and pilgrims on the earth, and they were looking for the next city because God had prepared a city for them. Imagine driving from North Carolina to California on I-40. Your one ambition in all of life is to see the Pacific Ocean. Half way through your journey, you pull off in

Oklahoma at a fishpond and decide that this is the Pacific Ocean. You would only be so stupid if you did not know where you were going. If it were not clear to you how vast the Pacific Ocean is, how beautiful the Pacific Coast Highway is, and how stunning a vision it presents, then you would be perfectly satisfied with the slimy, half-acre pond. There is nothing wrong with the pond—you might enjoy it along the way. But it is a part of the journey, not the destination.

Or imagine a runner rounding the track once, in a four-lap, one-mile race, and deciding he was done. This is the metaphor of the writer in chapter 12. Based on the fact that Abraham ran, based on the fact that all the others of chapter 11 ran, we are encouraged to "lay aside every encumbrance and the sin which so easily entangles us, and let us run with endurance the race that is set before us" (12:1). The analogy works. We are not running for the sake of running; we are running to win, and winning is defined by reaching the destination. This is clear from the stated objective of the running, which is running with endurance. The idea of endurance is that of bearing under something—a patient holding on. Since we have a destination in mind, we need to keep running.

It makes perfect sense that we would lose the sin that entangles us. Whatever runners need to succeed, they cannot have anything impeding their stride. This is the idea. Sin trips us and keeps us from being able to strive toward the destination. This is obvious. But the writer sees it more broadly than this. We are to lay aside not only the sin that entangles us but also the weights that keep us down. This is the encumbrance. It is interesting that the author does not put these things in the category of sin. There are some things that can weigh us down that are not necessarily sinful. Perhaps now is a time when we should expect some troubling applications: misplaced sexual desires, overindulgence in food, hobbies, entertainment, and we could go on making a long list until we felt as convicted as possible. The point is that by calling it a "weight," the writer is suggesting that anything that slows down our progress toward the goal of sanctification has to go. You can fill in your own list.

Whatever is on our list, it's just not worth it because it is slowing us down. It pulls at the wheel of our sanctification, causing us to exit too soon and stay a while, enjoying our weight. But this is a race. You don't stop in a race; you run to win. This is why Paul could write to Timothy that "no soldier in active service entangles himself in the affairs of everyday life, so that he may please the one who enlisted him as a soldier" (2 Tim. 2:4).

CONCLUSION

So, again, how do we manage our self-perception? Do we perceive ourselves as a frustrated prophet, a witty intellect, a pithy communicator, an orator, a CEO, a cultural iconoclast, a salesman, a cloistered monk with justifiably weak social skills, or perhaps we just simply want to be the coolest guy people know.

In Romania, under the worst persecution, Christians were simply known as "repenters." It was a derogatory term meant to call out the low-life scum who dared to follow Christ. But this is a compliment. And this is who we are. We are repenters. We are redeemed rebels who are calling other rebels to be redeemed. We are no longer managing our image. No. We have thrown off our robes and are taking the long walk outside the city. We are looking up at the thrashed corpse and taking a stand—this is who we are! We are cross bearers because we are cross lovers.

No preacher can throw his voice and make people believe that he is in the room when he is not. Dear brother, if you are finding your identity in anything else but the shameful cross, please repent. We are not ventriloquists throwing our voices into an image that we have created. No. We must incarnate what we propagate. In this way, our mouths are moving but the voice is God's.

Honestly, many of the magazines that we Christians produce and conferences we compose often read like we have exited too soon. Whatever this life gives, whatever it offers, it is nothing compared to what is to come. The temptation for us preachers is to exit too soon. We get so enamored with our earthly identity that we lose perspective.

How often have I been guilty of thinking where I want to fit in the church culture, all the while wondering how I need to act and think to be so accepted? We can't call people to a heavenly city when we preachers are all crowding ourselves into a roadside Stucky's comparing how good we have it in this life. We are so far from our destination. This life is not who we are. This is a journey, not a destination.

For this reason we should "run with endurance the race that is set before us" (12:2). Hebrews 13:14 contrasts our present "city" with the heavenly city, which will last, or endure. The idea is that we endure through this present city because this city does not endure. It's not that this life is all bad. There is much to be enjoyed that draws glory to Christ. But don't pull off. Don't exit too soon.

[6]

Imitate

Communicating the Example of Christ

We cannot communicate Christ without first imitating the communication of Christ and emptying ourselves so that He can live through us.

*Have this attitude in yourselves which was also in Christ Jesus,
who, although He existed in the form of God, did not regard
equality with God a thing to be grasped, but emptied Himself.*
—Philippians 2:5–7a

The steely grip of grace unites my heart to God until I can feel no more pain than what He wants me to feel, experience no more love than what He has for me, and know no more than what He wants me to know.

But this laceration to the cross brings with it the disparity of my soul—it means that I must be emptied to God, completely abandoned. And nothing—absolutely nothing—is so against my nature as abandoning my nature. A dog prefers his cage, a lion prefers his bondage, and a man prefers his cell more than my flesh wants to abandon and surrender itself to God. Nothing makes this attractive. This is why Philippians 2:5–7 is such a challenging text. It declares that Christ set aside His rights; He surrendered them for us. In order for Christ to accomplish the will of the Father in saving us, He had to first lay aside His privileges. In this way, the preacher becomes a communicator of the gospel only after he has imitated Christ in this life of surrender.

In this chapter we will apply the text of Philippians 2 to preaching. This is appropriate, for surrendering, in imitation of Christ, is exactly what is demanded of us as preachers. It is precisely the means to the cross in the pulpit. Maybe it would be helpful to think of preachers as people trying to drive down the narrow road, all the while trying to get people off the broad road. So before we look at Philippians 2, perhaps a parable is in order.

A PARABLE

Life is a road that takes all people to God. All roads *do* lead to God. The difference is that when we get to God, we find that there are two destinations in God. There is wrath—a destination for those who have rejected God for another god, for those who have worshipped themselves, and for those who have worshipped the road. Wrath is God's response to those who have rejected the other road. While this seems harsh, remember that every person is free to choose his or her path. So if someone wants to drive hard and fast to wrath, the loving God will graciously offer another path, but He will not force them to make a U-turn.

The other destination in God is grace—unequalled grace, paradise, heaven. This destination is prepared for those who prepared for their journey, and it is just as sweet as wrath is vile. It is for those who understood they could not get to God on their own. They understood that there was another destination, and so they allowed God to put them on a road that leads to the destination of grace, not the destination of wrath.

This is the road I am on and that every true preacher is on, and it is peculiar for its view. This high road provides the only vantage point from which you can see all roads and both destinations. From this road I can look and visualize the destination of rejection and see the millions of roads that pour into that one road that leads to wrath. From this road I can see the road I am on—the simple, narrow, stretch of highway cluttered with a few undeserving pilgrims going on to grace. And I am fighting two things within me. The first is the temptation to exit and stop along the way. There are so many things to see as the road winds through life: hobbies, interests, pleasures. I must be really special since all of these things are vying for my attention.

The second temptation is quite the opposite. This is the temptation to roll up the tinted windows and turn up the Christian music so that I cannot see or hear the other road. (It is very hard to listen to the MP3s of my sermons with all that racket coming from the other road.) You see, the other road, the road to wrath, runs very close to the little, narrow road I am on. And no matter how much I look the other way, no matter how loud the music is, I just cannot get the other road out of my mind. Neighbors, friends, and family members are all on the other road—all traveling at a breakneck pace to that awful end. Billions of them are blazing along, and millions more are needing roadside assistance.

God help them. And God help me.

You see, in my gut I know that I should exit and help them. The problem is that sometimes the road I am on looks less attractive than the road they are on. So how can I honestly exit and ask them to come to something I am not confident in myself? And this is the reality that I have to face. Am I willing to exit to the other road without falling in love with it? It would be easier if I were just at the destination, but I'm not. I'm just here, wallowing in my insecurity and trying to keep my GPS on grace, while telling those heading toward wrath that they are not going toward grace.

And unless I am willing to surrender to this call on my life, I will never know that sweet joy of seeing someone exit off the road of wrath, have a complete overhaul, and ramp up toward grace.

So I exit.

There on the roadside is a perfect stranger who needs assistance. As I give him assistance (which in this case takes a very long time), I am talking about the other road and the two destinations, not because I am showing off but because my whole existence is framed by my understanding of the destination of grace and it just comes out.

"Aren't all the roads going to the same place?" he asks. This is a common malady of those going to wrath—they think they are going to grace. It is not clear to him that there actually is a difference in our two destinations, and I understand why. You see, grace is located just beyond wrath, so as one is traveling it appears that the roads lead to the same destination. As a result you hear this a lot on the other road. I exit at other times and talk to my friend some more. He is running more smoothly now; and while I am happy that he is doing well, I fear that his good progress will only speed him down to wrath much faster.

He simply is not convinced of the two-destinations theory. And really, I cannot blame him for this. Remember, you can only see both roads and the two destinations from the narrow road. From all the other roads, the narrow road looks like just one more road, only harder to drive on and filled with a lot of weirdoes, nut jobs, and paranoid isolationists. It's not until the roads end that one sees that the narrow road is longer. It is composed of a material that allows it to span over wrath and arrive at grace. But when you see this, it's too late. Once you are at wrath, you cannot span it; you can only go in. The only way my friend can avoid wrath is if he is awakened to see the two roads.

One day I'm driving, minding my own business, when some punk cuts me off. Road rage is not uncommon on the narrow road, but I try to control myself. It is obvious that this guy does not know how to drive. I will patiently pull around him and leave him safely behind me. I could pull up to him and offer help, but he seems like he is new to the road. And new drivers on the narrow road are always careless, so excited about the destination that they run everyone over. And there he is.

At first, I thought I had exited to see him, but no, he was on *my* road, our road. The one I had exited to help was now gladly on the road to grace! We pull over and chat. It seems that as he was rebuilding his car (again) one day, he was thinking about what I said, and he thought he could see. He could not really see the narrow road, but in his mind's eye, he could conceive of it; and considering the destination of wrath, he decided to believe, to exit and permanently travel the narrow road. He was scared. He was insecure. But so was I when I first learned to drive on the narrow road. And oddly, while I really believed in grace, now that I have helped someone find the road, I'm more confident about the destination than ever.

This is Christianity, and this is preaching: driving down one road and trying to get people to exit the road to wrath and enter the road of grace. All metaphors break down and in that way are weak tools for theology. But inasmuch as they open the mind's eye, perhaps they can help us see a difficult truth, a truth as difficult as Philippians 2.

EXPOSITION OF PHILIPPIANS 2:5–11

The church at Philippi was in conflict. In order to counter this bickering spirit, Paul encourages the Philippians to make his joy complete by

> being of the same mind, maintaining the same love, united in spirit, intent on one purpose. Do nothing from selfishness or empty conceit, but with humility of mind regard one another as more important than yourselves; do not merely look out for your own personal interests, but also for the interests of others. (Phil. 2:2–4)

Paul is trying to illustrate the point that for them to accomplish God's purposes, they had to think that others were more important than themselves. Selflessness, abandonment of their own desires for the desires of others—these were the ideals that he wanted them to grasp. However, his commands, like all communication, were limited without an example, a metaphor. So Paul, the rhetorically astute theologian, decides to use the most extreme example of selflessness ever found. He uses the example of Christ Himself. Paul encourages his readers to have the same attitude in them that was in Christ, who, "although He existed in the form of God, did not regard equality with God a thing to be grasped, but emptied Himself" (vv. 6–7a).

Paul's description of Christ's *ekenosen*, or emptying, is a source of textual and theological debate. The chief concern is exactly how Christ "emptied" Himself. For years church leaders debated the issue of exactly how Christ was incarnated as a man. Did this mean that Christ stopped being God when He came to earth? This certainly seems to be against the biblical witness. Some suggested that while He was God He simply did not have divine omniscience, omnipotence, or omnipresence. However, this does not resolve the issue. Logically, God is defined by those qualities and more; so if Christ is God, He would have to have all of those qualities. If the "emptying" meant that He was no longer all-knowing or all-powerful, then He was *not* God.

While Christ took on the form of a human, He set aside His rights as God. In other words, all of Christ's time on earth He was always Godlike. When He was tired in Samaria, He was all-powerful; when He was asking questions in the temple, He was all-knowing; and when He was present in a particular place, He was omnipresent. It is simply that He made a choice not to take hold of what was always, and always will be, His—namely, His Godlike properties.

Imagine that you are visiting a hospital. You cannot find a parking place close to the hospital, so you park way in the back, and now you are lost. You stop another driver in the lot to ask directions, and he kindly says that he will just park beside you and walk with you to where you need to be in the hospital. Now suppose that as you get to the front of the hospital, you find out that this man is actually the chief surgeon of the hospital, and as you near the door, he adds, "Oh, yes, and this is my parking place." He had a superior advantage because of his status. However, in deference to your needs, he did not take his rightful parking spot but walked with you the whole way. So here is the question: As he was walking with you, did he stop being a doctor? No. Did he have a parking place? Yes. He had all of these things and at any time could have laid hold of those things and used them, but for your sake he just chose not to in that particular moment.

As thin as that metaphor is, it exists above only to illustrate that Christ's walking among human beings did not mean He was not God. Then why did He not reverse His tiredness or overcome all His physical limitations? It is because if He were to override His humanity, He would not have been fully in the form of a man and therefore could not fully empathize with our weakness or save us by His perfect life. The Incarnation was not just an event at Bethlehem. The Incarnation was the moment-by-moment choice of Christ to lay down His privileges, His rights as God, and to acquiesce to ungrateful sinners every second in order to effect our salvation.

In essence, Christ concealed Himself so that He might reveal the Father. Thus the veiling of Christ's full identity was necessary for God to be known fully. In the same way the Christian preacher's "rights" are willfully suspended in an effort to reveal the Father, Christ's emptying was a necessary means of accomplishing the communication of the Incarnation. Preaching can only veil God or the preacher; if the preacher is not veiled, then God will be. Thus the preacher must be tied to the text in a way that hides himself and throws light upon God through the Scripture. As Francois Fénelon noted, "The good man seeks to please only that he may urge justice and the other virtues by making them attractive. He who seeks his own interest, his reputation, his fortune, dreams of pleasing only that he may gain the bow and esteem of men able to satisfy his greed or his ambition."[1]

The divesting of oneself of rights, privileges, and status seems particularly foreign to what any human, preacher or not, desires. The natural desire of a preacher is to consummate the call of God within the pride of his ability. This position is antithetical to Christian preaching for the very reason that the proclamation of the Word of God cannot be separated from its means. There is no separation between the means of communication, Christ incarnate, and the message He

---

1. Francois Fénelon, *Dialogues on Eloquence*, trans. Wilbur Samuel Howell (Princeton, NJ: Princeton University Press, 1951), 62.

came to preach.[2] Christ came to say that one must die to himself and then find life in Him. The medium in which He spoke those words was a broken, humble spirit of an individual who, in reality, laid claim to all that existed. Christ's method did not veil but rather facilitated the message of the gospel. The message Christ preached was modeled in the way that He preached it. Can Christian preaching do any less?

All internal desires for wealth, fame, attention, accolade, praise, or comfort fight the very message preached. When a sinful spirit carpets the heart of the preacher, the most faithful explanation of the Word is drowned. It defeats the purpose of God. And, if God will not use this type of man, then neither cunning exegesis nor contemporary application can compensate.

Surrender

Remember that Christocentric communication is perfect. Paul made clear in 2 Corinthians 4:4 that people are in the dark and only Christ turns the light on; therefore if we preach ourselves, people will stay in the dark. This is true because the Father is revealed in Christ and Christ in the Word. Therefore, we must preach the Word, which will reveal Christ, who always points to the Father. Now here is the kicker. Not only must we declare Christ from the Word with the same faithfulness that Christ reflected the Father, but we must do so in the same way. The only way for Christ to fully communicate the Father was to fully abandon accessing the privileges that were His own.

So there is no way around it. If I am to communicate Christ the way Christ communicated the Father, then I have to surrender my privileges in the same way.

As preachers we understand this from our own sermons as we apply this text. We say to the high school student, "Die to your right to be popular so that you can follow Christ." We say to the businessman, "Die to your right to advance yourself financially so that Christ can

---

2. Compare Marshall McCluhan's suggested relationship between the message and medium of communication. The Christological application of McLuhan's thought is a subject worthy of further explanation.

be communicated through your integrity." Now the tough question: What do we preachers have to die to so that Christ can live in us? What is it that will keep us from exiting and telling people about the second destination called grace? In the next chapter we will argue that after a preacher is surrendered to God as Christ was surrendered to the Father, then he will have to be surrendered to the text, surrendered to the audience, and surrendered to excellence in preaching.

Decoding God

Throughout the sixteenth and seventeenth centuries, scholars made multiple attempts to decipher ancient Egyptian hieroglyphics. In the late 1800s Napoleon captured Egypt, and in 1877 French soldiers began an effort to build a fort for Napoleon. In the process one of the soldiers, Pierre-Francois Bouchard, unearthed a block of black basalt stone, later to be named the Rosetta Stone. It measured three feet nine inches long, two feet four and half inches wide, and eleven inches thick, and it contained three distinct bands of writing. The bands etched on the stone were three languages: on the top was hieroglyphics, and Dometic in the middle, followed by Greek on the bottom. Hieroglyphics were common in Egypt, but to date no one was able to decipher the mysterious language. While the historical value of the middle Dometic was uncertain, researchers quickly realized that the names of royalty in the bottom Greek text corresponded to similar characters in the cartouches within the hieroglyphics. After twenty years Jean-Francois Champollion broke the code and deciphered the meaning of the hieroglyphics. The language could not be understood apart from a translating language.[3]

On the Rosetta Stone of the Word of God, Christ is the translating language. One reads Scripture and ponders the hieroglyphics of a God who would love Israel, destroy Sodom in wrath, and create man in wisdom. He is beyond comprehension. Yet on the pages of the same

---

3. Richard A. Strachen and Kathleen A. Roetzel, *Ancient Peoples: A Hypertext View*, http://www.mnsu.edu/emuseum/prehistory/egypt/hieroglyphics/rosettastone.html (accessed September 8, 2006).

book is God's Speech, Jesus Christ. In His humanity He decoded the God who was beyond our comprehension. Thus, the bottom Greek of Christ translates for us the top hieroglyphic of God.

CONCLUSION

So I learned some lessons on the road. The first is that people don't come on to the narrow road unless we are willing to exit and communicate with those going to wrath. I *must* exit. The second is that if I stay on the exit ramp, I start to like the other roads and lose my passion for the narrow road. And then, in heartbreaking irony, my attempts get *no one* to the narrow road. It's as if leaving the road is leaving a comfort zone for the unknown—a sacrifice that must be made to get others going toward grace. So I have to find a way for my life to intersect with the other roads—without loving the other roads but loving those on the other roads.

I know that God wants those on the other roads to be on the narrow road. But the same God wants me to exit. And when I do, and when someone comes onto the narrow road, this brings true assurance. It's as if I accepted a place called grace, but when I led someone onto the narrow road, I truly believed in grace. So this is the third lesson: if I don't exit, I will never see them come to grace, I will not enjoy my road to grace, and I will never have full confidence that I am going to grace as well. The great motivation for purity of life, the great compelling reason that I should not fall in love with the other roads, the great reason that I should abandon my rights to drive however I want, is that a person in love with the other roads is hardly compelled to bring them from the other roads to the narrow road. The only ones who can know they are going to grace are the ones who spend time exiting without falling in love with the exits.

It's all in how you exit.

Part 3

The Cross and the Pulpit Ministry

*Surrendering to Christ
in the Preaching Task*

A cross in the pulpit means a death—a surrender. Specifically, the preacher will need to surrender to the text he is preaching. He must not be exalted above it but submitted to it. He will also have to surrender to the audience. Their need to know the truth is more important than his desire to preach the truth. Finally, the cross in the pulpit demands surrender to the task of great preaching.

[7]

Surrendered to the Text

The first surrender demanded of a preacher is
a commitment to proclamation not invention—
the commitment to preach the text alone.

*Certain zealous preachers who, under a pretext of apostolic simplicity,
do not deeply study either the doctrine of the Scripture or the marvelous
way God teaches us in it to persuade men. They imagine that they have
only to scream and to speak often of the devil and hell. It is unquestion-
ably necessary to strike people with living and terrible images; but it is
from the Scripture that one learns how to make these powerful effects.
One also learns admirably from it the way to make instructions con-
crete and popular, without making them lose the weight and power they
ought to have. Lacking these insights, the preacher often does no more
than daze the people. Distinct truths do not stay in their minds, and
even their awareness of fear is not lasting. The simplicity that he affects
is often an ignorance and vulgarity that try the patience of God. Nothing can excuse such men but the honesty of their intentions. . . . It is
much easier to paint the disorders of the world than to explain soundly
the basis of Christianity. For the former, one needs only to be experienced in the doings of the world and to be able to command language.
For the latter, a serious and profound contemplation of the sacred Scripture is required. Few men know religion well enough to explain it well.*

—Francois Fénelon

Epigraph. Francois Fénelon, *Dialogues on Eloquence*, trans. Wilbur Samuel Howell (Princeton, NJ: Princeton University Press, 1951), 135.

I have a vivid memory of kneeling in the choir room of a small country church in central Virginia, an hour's drive from my college campus. The little room had a few metal chairs sprinkled randomly throughout. I remember telling God that this was really all I had, so I begged Him to bless what was about to take place: my first sermon. I also remember my best friend with his arm around me, kneeling there coaching me graciously through this mix of nerves and fear. I remember the name of the sermon, the name of the pastor who let me preach, and the name of the little town. I remember a dozen other little details from that day. What I don't remember, as hard as I try, is the text from which I preached. There could be many reasons for this, but the one that haunts me is that the text simply was not the most important issue. In fact, it was not even an essential detail. I remember begging God that I would not blow it, that people would be saved, and that I would preach with passion and conviction. I do not remember asking God that I would be faithful to the text He had called me to preach. Why is this?

Well, with everything else going on, who had time to be concerned about explaining the text accurately? There was a hoard of details that must come together for this to be a "good" sermon. To get flustered over the technical realities of Scripture would be a distraction and an unnecessary burden. I am not trying to be self-deprecating. I am only saying that in retrospect it is very clear that in my mind the effectiveness, the quality of the sermon, had very little to do with the quality of the exposition. While this is a natural temptation, if indeed we are to bear a cross in the pulpit, and if this means that we are imitating the surrender of Christ, then at the very least we must be surrendered to the text when we preach. Not standing above the Word, or even beside the Word, but standing under it, in humility, is the only posture for those who will bear the cross in the pulpit.

We argued from Philippians 2 that a preacher must die to his rights so that the Word of God might live in others. The question now remains, to what must we surrender or die so that others might live? In this and the following chapters, we will explore the three surrenders of preaching: surrender to the text, surrender to the audience, and surrender to the task of great preaching. When a preacher is dying—is surrendering so that others might live—we will call this *surrendered communication.*

Surrendered communication is a relinquishing of our right to say anything we want any way we want. It is limiting our own freedom of expression in order to maximize effectiveness and minimize self-interests. What, then, is surrendering to the text? Surrendering to the text is at all times deferring to the Scripture, to the point that the sermon is always an expression of the content and spirit of a particular passage. The mental picture is of a preacher standing on the Word while simultaneously staying under the Word. John MacArthur writes, "The preacher who brings the message people most need to hear will often be the preacher they least like to hear. But anything less than a commitment to expository preaching by the preacher will reduce his sheep to a weak vulnerable, and shepherdless flock."[1]

In John 15:7 Jesus said, "If you abide in Me and My words abide in you, ask whatever you wish, and it will be done for you." This is the wonderful promise of God's attendance to the prayers of those whose lives are submitted to His will. The word translated "abide" in the NASB is *meno,* meaning simply to stay or remain. The believer who remains under the authority of the Word will ask in accordance with God's will and for His kingdom, thus securing a positive response from the Father. The analogy to preaching is that of the preacher who stays under the Word—he does not move from it. He abides there. The promise of the blessing of the Father is not automatic. It is bequeathed in response to a heart that is permanently residing under the will of God. Similarly, God has not promised to bless the persuasive meanderings of the pulpit—no matter how cunning, no matter how brilliant the delivery or how perfect the timing. The only message that carries the promise of lifesaving results is the message that is forever tied to the text.

---

1. John MacArthur Jr. and the Master's Seminary Faculty, *Rediscovering Expository Preaching* (Dallas: Word, 1992), xvii.

Throughout the next three chapters, I will borrow freely from François Fénelon's *Dialogues on Eloquence*. Fénelon was a seventeenth-century French prelate, and *Dialogues on Eloquence* was one of the most important books on preaching at the time, and of all time. Written as a conversation between three characters, simply named A, B, and C, Fénelon shows concern that the contemporary French pulpit did not stay faithful to the text of the Scripture. In the *Dialogues* he deals with this directly when he challenges a sermon that had "false applications of Scripture," a sermon where the preacher "contented himself merely with finding a verbal affinity between the text and today's ceremony."[2] Fénelon goes on to ask, "Should he not have begun by understanding the true sense of the text before he applied it to his subject?"[3] This chapter will include three issues regarding surrendering to the text of Scripture: preaching for the long term, the power of precision, and persuasion without proof. So, while I take exception with the force of Fénelon's theology and the progression of his Catholic mysticism, his rhetorical theory is helpful in trying to make our point.

PREACHING FOR THE LONG TERM

A. Thus most sermons are the reasonings of philosophers. Sometimes we only cite the Scripture as an afterthought for the sake of appearance or ornament. Then it is no longer the word of God; it is the word and contrivance of men.

C. You agree that such men work to cast out the cross of Christ.[4]

From experience, preachers may find a cycle running through the course of their pulpit ministry. The cycle may begin with a congregation that may not have a healthy appetite for text-centered preaching.

---

2. Fénelon, *Dialogues on Eloquence*, 59.
3. Ibid.
4. Ibid., 135.

The preacher then finds himself in somewhat of a quandary. On the one hand, if the sermon stays close to the text and explains Scripture, he runs the risk of boring the people. Who in today's culture can bear up under the necessary textual ideas when so much else is going on in the world? On the other hand, he may make the exposition of the text a secondary concern and strive to be more compelling through the use of story, humor, and illustration. The yield of the second choice is a better response from the congregation, even if their understanding of the text is not accurate. Obviously this is a false dichotomy. We do not have to choose between these two ends. The most compelling preaching is that which finds its foundation in the text.

However, here is the problem. If I make my concern the primacy of the text, I may have to give up short-term results—the "oohs" and "aahs" that are so gratifying. I may not generate the emotional response so necessary in making a challenging job rewarding. I may not hear the "attaboys" that employees in my congregation hear from time to time at work for a job well done. It is possible that being faithful to the Scripture may mean not receiving the result of "stirring" people or having them walk the aisle. Of course I am not suggesting that we should not preach for immediate life change. Nor am I suggesting that we should not invite people to respond. I am suggesting that the genuine litmus test of real life change is permanence, faithfulness. What will these changed lives look like over time? The answer to this question will be determined largely by the believer's absorption of the meat of the Word.

If immediate emotional response is the primary goal of preaching, then it logically misses the significant point of preaching: long-term results. Jesus' parable of the soils in Mark 4:1–20 is especially relevant:

> He began to teach again by the sea. And such a very large crowd gathered to Him that He got into a boat in the sea and sat down; and the whole crowd was by the sea on the land. And He was teaching them many things in parables, and was saying to them in His teaching, "Listen to this! Behold, the

sower went out to sow; as he was sowing, some seed fell beside the road, and the birds came up and ate it up. Other seed fell on the rocky ground where it did not have much soil; and immediately it sprang up because it had no depth of soil. And after the sun had risen, it was scorched; and because it had no root, it withered away. Other seed fell among the thorns, and the thorns came up and choked it, and it yielded no crop. Other seeds fell into the good soil, and as they grew up increased, they yielded a crop and produced thirty, sixty, and a hundredfold." (vv. 1–8)

Jesus' explanation of the parable followed with these words:

The sower sows the word. These are the ones who are beside the road where the word is sown; and when they hear, immediately Satan comes and takes away the word which has been planted in them. In a similar way these are the ones on whom seed was sown on the rocky places, who, when they hear the word, immediately receive it with joy; and they have no firm root in themselves, but are only temporary; then, when affliction or persecution arises because of the word, immediately they fall away. And others are the ones on whom seed was sown among the thorns; these are the ones who have heard the word, but the worries of the world, and the deceitfulness of riches, and the desires for other things enter in and choke the word, and it becomes unfruitful. And those are the ones on whom seed was sown on the good soil; and they hear the word and accept it and bear fruit, thirty, sixty, and a hundredfold. (vv. 14–20)

Jesus is preaching to a large crowd. The seashore is so thick with flesh that He climbs into a boat, where the water would carry His voice and where He could create some space between Himself and the people. As He looks over the crowd, He explains that their lives are like dirt, the kind of dirt in which a farmer would plant seed. The Word of God was like seed planted in their hearts. Several aspects of this parable help us understand why the preacher should preach the text. Specifically, we will note what Jesus said, the way He said it, and what He did not say.

First, the entire point of Jesus' parable is to explain that *people react to the Word differently.*

The first type of soil represents those who don't get the Word directly—the seed fell off to the side and was just sitting there for the birds to come and eat. Jesus said the seed was sown to these, but the Word was picked up by Satan. This is just a reality that every preacher must deal with. There are those who will entertain the idea of following the Word, but they get distracted. The Enemy comes and derails them—he steals the seed before it can take root.

Then, there are those who really respond to the Word immediately, but they fail to grasp the deep implications of discipleship. The long-reaching tentacles of the faith have not seeped deep into their hearts where real change is made. They are excited about the Word; it just doesn't last. The temporal excitement of hearing about Christ does not outlast the frustrations and discouragements of life. So they lose it. They don't hang on. They are like seed that falls on rock—it shoots up but dies just as fast for lack of root. The sun comes up, and it gets fried. It's the same old problem—no roots.

Another type of person hears the Word but just can't seem to get past all the distractions of life. "The worries of the world, and the deceitfulness of riches, and the desires for other things enter in and choke the word, and it becomes unfruitful" (v. 19). These are the people who get it; they understand. However, the Word cannot compete with all the stuff of life. The ball games, work, travel, family life, money—all those things choke out the Word like a little plant trying to grow in a thornbush. In a provocative commentary on this type of soil, Jesus said they do not take root because of "desires for other things." The desire for the Word cannot contend with a desire for all the other competing passions of life.

Finally, some receive the Word, get it, and produce fruit. They are like fruit trees that grow up and produce bushels of fruit, healthy and strong. They can stand what life brings because their soil is rich and the roots are deep. This is what every preacher longs for but sees too little: soil that receives the Word and just takes off growing, so unmistakably aided by the grace of God.

So what makes the difference in the soils? The one seminal difference in the types of soil is duration. The real thing lasts. What is the difference between Peter, who denied, and Judas, who betrayed? Endurance. Peter repented, while Judas only regretted. The former died a martyr; the latter died a sinner. The true test of followership is endurance. Jesus said, "The one who endures to the end, he will be saved" (Mark 13:13). Jesus' words were not an admonition to take a vice grip on God or forfeit salvation. Rather, this was an observation. Those who endure give evidence of a genuine salvation that has taken eternal root within them.

The point of walking through this familiar passage is to observe Jesus' resolute confidence in His power to keep people. He knew that once people are truly born again, they cannot lose what God has given them. This is why preaching the text just makes sense. The text is the seed. If the seed is ever to get to the soil, it must be sown. The seed of the Word will have long-term effects on the proper soil. Therefore, if the test of salvation is long-term results, and the seed of the Word is what produces the long-term results, then reason dictates that preaching for real life change will be preaching that exposes people to Scripture over a sustained period so that they can experience genuine salvation, a salvation that will become obvious as they mature over time.

Second, it is important to note that *Jesus shared this parable at a time when a large crowd was gathering.* It is almost as if He were saying, "Look, you are following Me by the thousands. That's fine. But your presence here is pointless unless it bears long-term results." Call it guts, or call it chutzpah—Jesus had it. How else could we explain standing in front of a large crowd, the seeming objective of the whole preaching ministry, and saying "You only get it if you hang around"?

Why was Jesus so pointed? Why didn't He wow the crowd with oratory and just hope they would stick it out? The answer is twofold. First, it seems Jesus was trying, as He did on other occasions, to let them know that not everyone who follows is a true disciple. The test of true discipleship is always endurance. The implication is reminiscent of other words of Christ:

> Not everyone who says to me "Lord, Lord," shall enter the kingdom of heaven, but he who does the will of My Father who is in heaven will enter. (Matt. 7:21)

> Abide in Me, and I in you. As the branch cannot bear fruit of itself unless it abides in the vine, so neither can you unless you abide [remain] in Me. (John 15:4)

Second, Jesus is fore-telling as well as forth-telling. His prophetic voice was not only a challenge to those standing around but also a word about what was to come. They all heard the word that day, but only a few were left after His crucifixion and resurrection. It was clear that the seed took root in only a few hearts. If the symbolic seed took root in only one of four hearts, one might ask why one should work so hard for only a 25 percent return on all the effort. The answer, of course, is that the sower never really knows which seed will take root. The sower, then, must sow and keep on sowing with the humble admission that he does not know which seed will take root, because he does not know the condition of each type of soil.

Finally, it is interesting that *Jesus does not ask or answer the question about the culpability of the sower* for sowing on bad soil. Think about it. It seems the sower bears a little responsibility for throwing this seed all over the place—beside the road, on rocks, and especially among the thorns. Yet, Jesus never condemns the sower. In fact, He just assumes that a sower will distribute seed on places where it will not grow. Why? Well, the rocky soil that farmers in first-century Palestine had to cultivate was less than ideal. Don't think of the rich black soil of America's Midwestern farming communities. Think of little more than a rocky desert environment. It's not ideal, not well suited for sowing. Yet this is exactly Jesus' point. The sower does not wade through the ground picking the perfect spot. He treats every piece of earth as if it were perfectly capable of bearing fruit. This is the farmer's humility—he sows on all the soil indiscriminately. The farmer admits that seed will grow in the right conditions. Rain, sun, and time produce fruit. However, the farmer is completely ignorant of which seed will fall in the exact place to produce fruit. So his strategy is simple. Sow seed in every possible place. Expect that every seed sown is going to produce fruit.

Jesus is implying that the preacher rarely knows how the seed is going to take root. Every preacher would admit that there was an individual soil that looked promising, yet the seed did not make it through the first little storm. Other soil looked forever lost, yet it produced fruit of untold proportions. How many stories can we retell of great men and women used of God, who started out as the most unlikely candidates for fruitful lives? The preacher's strategy is simple: sow seed everywhere and in every place. This is the preacher's humility. While the preacher knows that seed will produce fruit in certain conditions, he is unaware of when and where the conditions will be right to produce such fruit.

The point is that preaching the Scripture is preaching for the long run. It is humble deference to the text. In humility the preacher must have utter confidence in the Word to produce lasting change over time. A farmer does not sow, cultivate, and harvest in one day. Rather, it is a process, a process of long-term sowing and cultivating of what has been sown, so that at harvesttime there is a joy in what God has produced in the heart through the Word.

THE POWER OF PRECISION

The essential skill that every preacher must hone is precision. This is the ability to say exactly what the text is saying with force and unction, while saying only what the text says—no more and no less.

An example of seemingly "accurate but imprecise" language is the phrase "Jesus died on the cross to pay the penalty for sin." This is a true statement. However, the problems with this statement to the average audience are many. First, a contemporary audience probably will not know what to do with this statement. They have trouble with the whole idea of sin in the first place, not to mention the mystery as to why Jesus would die for them. The second problem with this statement is with the churched audience. Most likely, they have heard this phrase so many times and in so many different contexts that it has lost its meaning.

In fact, if this phrase is used in place of a full understanding of the substitutionary atonement, then it is fair to say that the phrase is so imprecise that it misrepresents the truth. Jesus did die for our sins, but there is much more. When we realize the justice of God that, by virtue of His perfection, can never be compromised; the sacrifice of Christ in His incarnation and ultimate humiliation on the cross; the fact that Jesus became as sin so that we could live as innocents; and that the Father was willing for the penalty of my sin to be poured out on Him in a strange alchemy of love and justice, then we realize the truth is not only richer than "Jesus died for our sins," but it becomes something almost entirely different altogether. Speaking of the redemption perspective of the atonement, Leon Morris writes,

> Man belongs to God. God set him in Eden to live in fellowship with him. But man sinned. Man became the slave of evil. He cannot break free. . . . If I can say it irreverently, God, if he wants us back, must pay the price. And the great teaching of the New Testament is that God has paid the price. He has redeemed us. . . . We were in captivity. We were in the strong grip of evil. We could not break free. But the price was paid and the result is that we go free.[5]

---

5. Leon Morris, *The Atonement* (Downers Grove, IL: InterVarsity Press, 1983), 120–21.

Other concise ways to express this truth might be: "Jesus took the deathblow of God's anger against sin," "The death of Jesus satisfied the wrath of God against sin," "Jesus took the blow of God's anger so that we would not have to," or "Jesus was treated like a sinner so that God could treat us like innocents." These are not necessarily the best expressions of this truth, but the idea is to avoid expressions that so limit the truth that they inadvertently rob the listener of the joy flowing from the incredible truth of Christ's sacrifice for the sinner. Simply, there is too much rich truth in the idea of the atonement to be reduced to a phrase that, while convenient, does not convey the meaning of the passion of Jesus.

Why Is Precision Important?

Throughout the day we depend on sources of information that are not necessarily precise. "The putt breaks two feet to the right"; "It's about two o'clock"; "Your car may need a new air filter." If any of these pieces of information is off a little, the consequences are negligible. There is no harm done. We can recover from a lack of precision in these circumstances.

However, in some circumstances, precision is vital. You would not want to hear a doctor say, "You have cancer in your lung or in your brain; we just can't tell." You would not want to hear, "You may have a crack in the foundation of your house, but there is no way to know." If you cannot find the information right then, you keep seeking and seeking until you find the information that is exactly precise because the problem has serious consequences. In other words, *the need for precision depends upon the consequences of the truth*. In fact, if a lawyer were intentionally imprecise in a court of law, it could be a crime with severe legal ramifications. If his defense is that he was close to being right, the crime is all the more serious because he knew that the truth was in there somewhere but did not bother to extract the *exact* truth.

Similarly, when the preacher handles the Word, he is handling something that is more important than all the previously mentioned issues. More important than health or property is the understanding of God's expectation of, and love for, mankind. We must be precise. Anything less is misrepresentation of the eternal truth. It is not enough to get close or to be confident that the truth is in there somewhere. While we strive for force and clarity, we must simultaneously strive for accuracy.

Why this insistence on precision? The primary reason is that when we handle Scripture, the congregation generally believes that they are hearing what God has to say on a particular topic. It could be that the reason people think God is so glaringly irrelevant is because preachers have glossed over doctrinal truths in a way that makes them bland and unappealing.

Let us return to our example of the atonement. It may seem natural and appropriate to preach a sermon on the love of God and include the fact that Jesus died for sinners. However, if the preacher does not take pains to explain, at least in some fashion, the power of the atonement and the fact that the love that is inherent in God's essence drove Him to make this incredible sacrifice, then the real punch, the real meaning of the atonement, is lost.

If the brutal sacrifice is not presented in a way so compelling that the audience could never forget, then this simply is not precise. Why? Because the atonement *is* compelling. The cross *is* a spectacular display of love almost grotesque in its stubborn application, a love that wrapped one hand like a vice around the perfection of holy justice and the other around the vile imperfection of stinking flesh. Why be so graphic? Because it is graphic! Why try to be so persuasive? The truth is persuasive! If it is presented in any other way, then we are giving people the impression that the most powerful force in the world—God's saving power—is bland and boring, predictable, average, everyday. Yet, when the preacher takes pains to say with precision what the text is saying, it is compelling to say the least.

At the risk of overstatement, I will go so far as to say that in certain contexts the statement "Jesus died on the cross to pay the penalty for sin" is not true. It is not that a core truth does not exist;

rather, the problem is that in the statement's failure to carry the precise and glorious meaning of the theological truth, it emasculates the statement to the point of falsehood. If I had just lost my home and family in a fire and the person relaying the news to me says, "You lost your computer," that person would be giving me a statement that is true. If that is all the person told me, then it is a lie. It is a lie not in what the person says, but in what he or she does not say. *The indictment of contemporary preaching is not that it says wrong things but that it does not say right things clearly.* It does not lie; rather it veils glorious truths for the sake of expediency. The net result, however, is the same. The clichés that have reduced our theology for the sake of understanding now misrepresent our theology in their lack of precision.

Every preacher has a different style; and as the truth of the Word ebbs through personalities, it expresses itself differently. Some preachers are more passionate, some more compassionate, and others more practical. The sermon, of course, is shaped by who we are. However, how we present a certain text should not be wholly determined primarily by who we are but rather by what the text says.

Precise preaching of Luke's account of eternal damnation must reel with a certain horrifying pending reality for those who do not know Christ. It matters little if this offends my cultured sensibilities. It matters little if my audience is just too progressive to want to hear this type of sermon. It matters even less if I am not the kind of preacher who likes to get emotional. This is what the text says, and to represent it in any other way is to misrepresent Scripture. David's Psalm 23 account of the gentle Shepherd who leads us must be presented in a way that gives the real flavor of God's tender leadership. To scream through this text would simply misrepresent what David is saying. When we misrepresent the text, the congregation is missing this particular aspect of God's character and essence. Surely the presentation is influenced by style and personality. But we must be precise to the point that the mood of the text is reflected in the mood, or feel, of the sermon.

Now let us turn to the final aspect of surrendering to the text, the problem of persuasion without proof.

PERSUASION WITHOUT PROOF

What would you say of a man who persuaded you without proof? Such a one would not be a true orator. He might be able to seduce other men if he has the contrivances to persuade them without demonstrating that what he is inducing them to accept is truth. A man like that would be dangerous.[6]

Fénelon was concerned with the whole idea of persuasion. For Fénelon, exposition melded with persuasion made the preacher eloquent.[7] He was convinced that every form of art, and especially oratory, was inherently persuasive. The problem is that when you remove persuasion from exposition, you are left with a Bible lesson, not a sermon. When one removes exposition from persuasion, it leaves a persuasive message with no foundation in authority. In the end, it has no real bite, no staying power, and inherently no long-term effects because it is rooted in opinion and conjecture, not absolute truth.

Here is the temptation we preachers face: to be persuasive in a sermon without the proof of the persuasion. We are compelling yet on what authority? Charles Spurgeon wrote,

It is not true that some doctrines are for the initiated; there is nothing in the Bible that is afraid of the light. . . . Cautious reticence is, in nine cases out of ten, cowardly betrayal. The best policy is never to be politic, but to proclaim every atom of the truth so far as God has taught it to you.[8]

---

6. Fénelon, *Dialogues on Eloquence*, 88.
7. This will be covered in more detail in the following chapter.
8. Charles Spurgeon, *Lectures to My Students* (Grand Rapids: Zondervan, 1977), 74–75.

The Matter of Style

It needs to be said that this is not an issue of style. Some people are naturally authoritative. I don't feel that I have that same authoritative tone. My "thus saith the Lord" simply doesn't carry the same punch as that of many others. However, that does not excuse me from being authoritative. My authority as a preacher does not come from the tone of my voice or my posture. Rather it comes from the mandate that I am called to hold forth the Word of life (Phil. 2:16). For the believer, the command is to stand on the firm foundation of the Word while holding the Word out. For the preacher, the implication is to stand on God's Word and preach it clearly, because God has not given us a spirit of timidity but of power (2 Tim. 1:7). I am under obligation to retain the standard of sound doctrine and guard the treasure God has put in my heart (2 Tim. 1:13–14). This mix of personality and call is best described in the classic words of Andrew Blackwood, when he wrote,

> [Preaching] has in it two essential elements, truth and personality. Neither of those can it spare and still be preaching. The truest truth, the most authoritative statement of God's will, communicated in any other way than through the personality of brother man to men is not preached truth. Suppose it written in the sky, suppose it embodied in a book which has long held in reverence as the direct utterance of God that the vivid personality of the men who wrote its pages has well-nigh faded out of it; in neither of these cases is there any preaching. And on the other hand, if men speak to other men that which they do not claim for truth, if they use their powers of persuasion or of entertainment to make other men listen to their speculations, or do their will, or applaud their cleverness, that is not preaching either. The first lacks personality, the second lacks truth. And preaching is the bringing of truth through personality. It must have both elements.[9]

---

9. Andrew Blackwood, *Lectures on Preaching* (Grand Rapids: Zondervan, 1950), 5.

The issue then is not style. Our temperament, personality, style of preaching, or congregational preferences will all have implications on the way we preach. Yet they will never change the mandate we have to be persuasive with the Word of God. This then begs the question: if we are called to be persuasive and we respond to that call, and yet we do not stand on the Scripture when we persuade, are we not persuading without proof?

The Matter of Authority

> Calculate for yourself what authority a man would have if he said nothing of his own devising and did nothing but follow and explain the thought of the word of God. Moreover he would be doing two things at once: in explaining the truths of Scripture, he would be interpreting its text, and would be habituating Christians to always see the relations between the meaning and the letter. What more is needed to accustom them to nourish themselves on this sacred bread![10]

The reality is that the whole nature of preaching is authoritative. Let's face it, you are standing there as an authority on what God thinks. It is prudent that the preacher not trump this authority. It is probably even expected that he play it down in an effort not to seem too caught up in the position and become self-absorbed. This is wise. However, this sensitivity should not, and does not, remove the reality that we are an authority on spiritual things. But the truth is that we have, or at least think we have, observed this authority abused because of the stereotype of the blustering reverend who wields his clerical status like a sheriff's badge rounding up any vice in earshot. Since those of us who preach have to deal with this caricature, we may wince at the prospect of seeing ourselves as authoritative. Even a modicum of self-awareness makes us reticent to accept the role of an authority. Yet while there is a part of us that quivers at this thought,

---

10. Fénelon, *Dialogues on Eloquence,* 134.

as if we have postured ourselves as something we are not, we can never remove the inherent mandate in the call—to stand and say, "This is what God says you must do." It's just there, like night follows day. We are speaking the Word of God. If that is not what we want to do, there may be other professions more suited for us. If we are called to preach, we must accept and be faithful to the authority of the pulpit that comes from the authority of the Scripture. Titus was a phenomenal example of the challenge inherent in the authority that comes from the pulpit.

Titus: A Case Study in the Authority of Scripture

Titus was a strong first-century preacher who was facing a pretty serious challenge. He came to Christ under the ministry of the apostle Paul and had traveled with him—they had a great relationship. Paul thought a great deal of Titus and spoke of him in glowing terms (cf. 2 Cor. 7:14–15; 8:16–17; 12:18). He was Paul's "true child" (Titus 1:4). Paul had so much confidence in Titus that after a missionary journey in Crete, he told him to stay "in Crete that [he] might set in order what remains" (Titus 1:5). This was no small feat. What remained to be done was to appoint elders and organize churches in the area, amid heavy resistance. Titus proceeded with strong opposition from the Jewish community and from people who were upsetting the church while teaching the Scripture for profit.

To complicate things further, Titus was not a Jew. The Jews, arguably the most zealous religious group of that time, were not about to listen to a foreign Gentile. This caused serious challenges for Titus. Remember, Titus was not a novice. He was strong, seasoned, and as prepared for this task as possible. Yet, even strong people face opposition. It is often suggested that the book of Titus is a response to a letter Titus wrote to Paul asking for advice. Regardless, Paul gives Titus the insight he needs to deal with the problem. He writes, "For the overseer must be . . . holding fast the faithful word which is in accordance with the teaching, so that he will be able both to exhort in sound doctrine and to refute those who contradict" (Titus 1:7–9).

Titus had several problems. The first was the growing believers who wanted to grow even more—what should he do with them? The second problem was those who were contradicting everything he said. But the biggest problem was that of authority. Where was he going to get the necessary authority to deal with these two matters? He was an outsider, a newcomer. Paul's response is insightful. He simply says, "Titus, hold on to Scripture like a vice." Why? No matter what Titus brought in terms of godly behavior and personal character, his only authority was Scripture. Titus was facing a major church scrap. Its only resolution was strong doctrinal preaching. This type of preaching could both grow the believer and challenge those who contradicted the Word. Titus's only resolve was to lean on—have confidence in—Scripture for resolution of the challenges to his authority.

It is interesting that God rarely calls the person who has the strongest leadership ability or the greatest voice—physically or socially. Rather He most often chooses to call those who are faithful. That being said, where does the pastor get the nerve to stand in the pulpit and tell others what they should or should not do? If he is not the most quick-witted or does not have the greatest leadership ability, is he not setting himself up? The authority comes from nothing more or less than Scripture. If we are not surrendered to the Scripture, then we are sitting ducks, waiting for the onslaught of the Enemy. We are defenseless. What's more, we are speaking with authority when we have no authority.

Again, there is a tendency to play down this authority by the style in which the preacher presents the Word. A casual tone seems to bid well with a congregation who is not looking for someone to speak at them but to them. God help us if we transpose the authority in preaching the Word to a personal authority, but let us not forget that there is authority in preaching. If we ignore the authority, even out of a sense of humble self-deprecation, there may be a tendency not to project the authority that is in the Word. If we ignore the authority in the Word while we preach, then we are simply persuading without proof, calling for life change without a foundation on which to build a life. Why is this so challenging in preaching? If there is a pendulum of pulpit abuse, it seems to have swung from the preacher who abuses his authority to the preacher who will not assume any authority at all.

The Matter of Truth

It is necessary here to say a word about the nature of the times in which we live. This is done with great hesitation, as the words *postmodernism, relativism,* and *pluralism* perhaps have been used and misused to the point of irrelevance. They carry little meaning anymore. So at the risk of being redundant, there are two points about the state of truth that are germane to this discussion.

First, we do live in challenging times. The idea of absolute truth left long ago. Preachers seemingly caught on to this sometime in the 1980s and began to challenge the notion from the pulpit with dead-on logic. After all, there must be truth because God said there is truth, so the preacher must persuade the congregation from their point of view to the "true" point of view. The problem was the congregation did not necessarily have a point of view. In fact, it seems that congregations mentally entertained themselves by comparing notes between news outlets, "soft news," daytime television, academic posturing, and what the preacher had to say. Few formed an opinion. It was just too mentally taxing and unimportant. It was not that the relative nature of truth was being competitively preached from another pulpit across town. Relativism simply oozed up from a growing, ground-level suspicion that not all these people could be right but certainly not all these people could be wrong either. Truth must belong to the individual.

It seems that eventually there will be a philosophical and then a cultural reaction to this postmodernism. Yet that day is not yet. Our pew sitters still grapple in the world of relativism and cultural subjectivity.

So how have we responded? It seems that the present trend is not to take on the illogic of postmodern thought but rather to ignore it or embrace it. The preacher knows that it exists, yet he has decided to hit people where they live. The preaching deals decidedly with the perceived needs of the congregation. Appropriate subjects are financial freedom, emotional stability, physical fitness, or psychological wholeness. And in an effort to "eat the fruit and spit out the seeds," congregations have embraced progressive presentations of these practically rooted messages.

The purpose of this discussion is not to challenge this approach but rather to make one observation—the second point here—relative to the topic of authority in preaching. While a conversation, much more a sermon, on the absolute nature of truth seems heavily passé in this age, it does not change the reality that the church is the protector and defender of the Word of God—period. No one else will do it. The social clubs, political organizations, and educational systems will not preserve the pure teaching of Scripture for the next generation. The Christian colleges and seminaries can be comparatively ineffective, because they represent relatively few of those who are coming into the church. And they are supported by the local churches, which, if not strong, cannot hold the schools accountable for truth. There is no one else who even pretends to do this. The church is it. Paul's admonition to Timothy, "Retain the standard of sound words which you have heard from me, in the faith and love which are in Christ Jesus. Guard, through the Holy Spirit who dwells in us, the treasure which has been entrusted to you" (2 Tim. 1:13–14), is even more relevant today.

In summary, if the church uses the perceived needs of people to get to the heart of their spiritual needs, then it is striking at a strategy used by Jesus Himself. However, if in addressing the perceived needs of people, the church ignores the authority of the Word, and thus the doctrines of the church, it will produce a generation that knows far too little to challenge falsehood and grapple with truth, since they have no basis for authority to do so. The bottom line is that preaching is both persuasive and authoritative. Preaching not centered on the authority of the Word by default takes its authority from the preacher. The authority of the preacher without the Scripture, while possibly entertaining, leaves the church ill equipped to deal with the continued onslaught that our children and their children will face.

CONCLUSION

In essence, we are called to re-present Scripture. The preacher's responsibility is to repackage it in a way that changes nothing of the flavor of the original presentation. Rather the re-presentation makes the listeners hungry for more of the original, to the point that they are not satisfied until they have sunk their teeth deeply into the original, eating to their hearts' content. Understandably, their appetite will wane. This is when they return to the table to digest the re-presentation in a way that makes the original irresistible.

I am amazed at how many times I face the subtle temptation to offer, without warning, my opinion alongside the authority of Scripture. While done innocently, it does not reflect a complete surrender to Scripture, a surrender that parallels surrender to God. The surrender of my will to God's will is a daily, hourly struggle. So in preaching, every sermon is a chance to show my love for Him by lifting His Word above mine and His authority above mine. Remember, we are not inventors; we are proclaimers.

This chapter may seem to argue for a pure "naked exposition." It may seem that I am arguing for those who simply get the text right, no matter how it is presented: cold, static, lifeless, boring preaching. No matter how much we appreciate their objective, they simply do not move the audience. Their preaching isn't compelling. It's simply boring preaching. There are boring expositors but probably just as many boring preachers who do not walk through a text of Scripture to explain it.

You can't blame boredom on faithfulness to Scripture. Scripture is exciting—the preacher brings the boredom. We will deal with this in chapter 9. For now it is enough to know that the text is primary.

Without it, the preacher can have a lot to say but say nothing at all that produces long-term results, precisely represents Scripture, or is authoritatively based on the Word of God.

[8]

Surrendered to the Audience

The good man seeks to please only that he may urge jus-
tice and other virtues by making them attractive. He who
seeks his own interest, his reputation, his fortune, dreams
of pleasing only that he may gain the bow and esteem of
men able to satisfy his greed or his ambition. Thus, even
his case can be reduced like that of the good man to per-
suasion as the single aim which a speaker has; for the self-
interested man wishes to please in order to flatter, and he
flatters in order to inculcate that which suits his interest.

—Francois Fénelon

But while the basic message thus remains constant and in-
variable, our presentation of it must take account of, and be
largely conditioned by, the actual world on which our eyes
look out to-day. The gospel is not for an age, but for all time:
yet it is precisely the particular age—this history's hour and
none other—to which we are commissioned by God to speak.
It is against the backdrop of the contemporary situation that
we have to reinterpret the gospel once for all delivered to the
saints; and it is within the framework of current hopes and
fears that we have to show the commanding relevance of Jesus.

—James Stewart

Epigraphs. Francois Fénelon, *Dialogues on Eloquence* (Princeton, NJ: Princeton University Press, 1951), 62; and James Stewart, *Heralds of God* (New York: Scribner's, 1946), 11.

A MODIFICATION OF PLATO

Imagine a cave. Within the cave are people chained with no way of escape. The people always have been chained there; they have never seen the outside. They have little concept of reality and cannot grasp all the things the normal person would hold as special or sacred. They have never seen a sunset or children at play; they have never even seen a crowded street with people walking about. It would be fair to say that they do not understand what we would call "reality"; in fact, their concept of reality is really framed by the subtle nuances that they gather from sound and shadow.

Now imagine that the people in the cave are seated with their backs to the entrance. Inside the cave is a small wall upon which silhouettes are cast, so that the prisoners' understanding of reality is warped by space and light. A small child may appear to be a giant, and a dog may appear to be a mammoth beast. If such a people did exist and there was no hope of loosening their chains, the only merciful thing for those outside the cave to do would be to go to them and describe the shadows they were seeing. The shadows would then be interpreted, and those in the cave would have a better sense of reality. Now, herein lies the problem.

Those outside the cave are accustomed to the light. Their reality is so constructed by a light world that they can hardly see in the dark. The only hope for those in the cave is that those on the outside find a way to see in the dark. If they could see in the dark and simultaneously retain their understanding of what was in the light, then they could communicate clearly what was in the light.

This, as you may already know, is a much-simplified borrowing from Plato's allegory of the cave.[1] Plato was attempting to illustrate the power of the republic and its influence upon those who did not understand the republic. However, with apologies to the ancient Greek rhetorician/philosopher, there is an application here to preaching.

---

1. Plato used his allegory of the cave to represent his epistemology of forms. He believed that all knowledge is a form of true knowledge. In his application he believed the philosophers should return to the cave to learn to see in the dark. It is very loosely borrowed here. See Plato's *Republic* in *Plato: Complete Works*, ed. John M. Cooper (Indianapolis: Hackett, 1997), 971.

The preacher is called to speak to those who are in darkness. The preacher, as a Christian, is living in the light. His whole construction of reality is built on the fact that he lives in and enjoys the light. He cannot conceive of a reality outside this light. While this is the glorious reality of one who is a believer, it presents a challenge for those who are in the cave. Ironically, those in the light have a hard time seeing in the dark. They have come out of the darkness; they hate the darkness, even to the point that it seems strange to enter a dark place from where they have been delivered. They would, if they could at all do so, remain in the light forever and never go into the dark place again.

However, this does not change the reality that there are still millions who are in the darkness. They do not know that they are in the darkness because it is the only reality they have ever known. Their understanding of what is really in the light is shaped by profoundly limited perceptions of spiritual voices they have overheard from other conversations and by the shadows of reality that appear in their dark cave. Due to this darkness, they are content to construct realities based on shadows. They treat this mortal world as if it were permanent and the immortal spiritual world as if it did not exist. Light to them is darkness, for who would want to be blinded by the piercing light that is so hard to live in. After all, living in the light just demands so much. The only reason they can think that someone would leave the security of the darkness for the blinding light is that they must be insecure. They deduce that there are those who do not have the tenacity to bear the issues of the darkness, so they gravitate to the light as a means of escape—abandoning the pure reality of the darkness to live in a fantasy world called light. It is quite amazing to those in the darkness that some poor, dependent souls would be so quick to call their light-world reality. Darkness is the reality. Light is the fantasy.

SEEING IN THE DARK

What is the preacher to do? Where is the preacher in this mix? Those in the light are so comfortable in the light that they do not want to leave. Those in the darkness are convinced that the shadows are the reality, not realizing the source of light that causes the shadows. The preacher, then, is one who sees in the dark. The authentic champions of light are not those who glibly relish their illumined status; rather it is those who squint. They are the light dwellers who return to the darkness to take reality to those who live in fantasy while thinking that it is reality. This is the preacher's task.

Perhaps the most compelling statement of this tension in which the preacher lives is the words of James Stewart in "The Preacher's World," the first chapter of his classic work on preaching, *Heralds of God*. Stewart writes,

> But this is not to say that the preacher must stand aloof, cultivating a spirit of detachment from the march of events . . . the real work of the ministry will not be done by any man who shuts himself in with his academic interests and doctrinal theorizing, as though there were no surge and thunder of world-shattering events beating at his door. Surely in this immensely critical hour, when millions of hearts are besieged by fierce perplexities; when so many established land-marks of the spirit are gone, old securities wrecked, familiar ways and habits, plans and preconceptions, banished never to return; when the soul is destined to meet, amid the crash of old beliefs, the ruthless challenge and assault of doubt and disillusionment; when history itself is being cleft in twain, and no man can forecast the shape of things to come—*the church needs men who, knowing the world around them, and knowing the Christ above them and within, will set the trumpet of the gospel to their lips, and proclaim His sovereignty and all-sufficiency.*[2]

It is easy to gather the mental image of the preacher who holes up in the study and resurfaces with a passionate word from God. That is a familiar picture because of the awareness that our passion for the

---

2. Stewart, *Heralds of God*, 12–13 (emphasis added).

Word grows from the place of discovery in the Word. There has yet to exist a preacher who was passionate about the Scripture in the pulpit whose heart first did not leap with the discovery of the richness of the text in the study. However, this passion for the text must be accompanied by compassion for the people.[3]

This is the tension in which the preacher lives: the tension between living in the light of the Word daily so that it emanates from the soul and clearly from the pulpit, and learning to see in the darkness of this world so that the words are not those of a student/scholar alone, but of a student/scholar/shepherd, a shepherd who smells like sheep. It was because the Pharisees could not see in the dark that Christ leveled the rebuke of John 10:11–15:

> I am the good shepherd; the good shepherd lays down His life for the sheep. He who is a hired hand, and not the owner of the sheep, sees the wolf coming, and leaves the sheep and flees, and the wolf snatches them and scatters them. He flees because he is a hired hand and is not concerned about the sheep. I am the good shepherd, and I know My own and My own know Me, even as the Father knows Me and I know the Father; and I lay down My life for the sheep.

This passage gives two compelling reasons why the preacher must be surrendered to people, why the preacher who loves his people is committed to both scholarship and compassion for people: first, it is the nature of the call; and, second, this is the model of our Lord.

THE NATURE OF THE CALL

This passage, in the context of what follows, is clearly a stab at the religious leaders of Christ's day. The preachers of Christ's day were all self-declared scholars. They had much of the Scripture committed to

---

3. Mark Copenger says that a preacher should be passionate (a function of emotion), dispassionate (a statement of confidence in the sufficiency of Scripture), and compassionate (a function of yearning for the souls of people).

memory and were insistent that the smallest infraction of the law be treated with the swiftest punishment. They were precise, exacting. They were passionate about Scripture. The problem was that they were more passionate about the text than they were toward those for whom the text was intended. They had greater love for the nuances of the text than for people.

But this is not an either/or proposition. It could be that you, as a preacher, have tremendous people skills. People just love you, and you love them. You praise those who speak of passion for people and wonder why those left-brained nerds spend all their time in the study while there are millions of people to be won to Christ. "Really," you wonder, "how many people are going to be saved by my ability to parse a Greek verb? The results, after all, speak for themselves. Since so many people are blessed by my ministry, it stands to reason that the 'people' approach is much better than the 'scholar' approach to ministry."

Conversely, it's possible to have such a love for the text of Scripture that your one passion is to study it, understand it, and distribute it from the pulpit. You relish the opportunity to spend quality time in the text alone, without interruption. On some occasions you have even strangely thought that ministry to people would be so great if it were not for all those people! People are blessed by your preaching/teaching, and you reason that so many people are blessed that this justifies the lack of disciples made by your personal witness and ministry.

But this is not an either/or proposition. We all have God-given strengths and weaknesses. The fact that God did not make you the perfect blend of pastor/teacher is not a statement of God's oversight. Rather, our limitations remind us of our imperfections against the backdrop of His perfection. This is His way of keeping us humble before Him. The scholar needs the grace of God in huge measure if he is to have a deep love for people. The people person needs a great measure of grace if he is to have the tenacity to stay in his chair until he has faithfully studied the text of Scripture. So be encouraged by this good-news/bad-news scenario.

The curse of our day may be the imbalance. Men gifted with people skills and administrative skills but who lack a high view of the sufficiency of Scripture are great at leading people, but one may ask where they themselves are being led, since the undershepherd does not take time to think deeply about Scripture. Conversely, there are those with a passion for being right about textual nuances but who lack missionary fire. They refuse to see in the dark. Their deft understanding of Scripture falls short of true communication since it never bridges the gap from first-century Palestine to the contemporary world. The challenging news is that we do not have the option. We must be scholars and lovers, students and friends, theologians and missionaries, readers and evangelists—people deeply saturated in the light who have learned to see in the dark. The good news is that whatever our inherent weakness, it is God's way of making us wholly dependent on Him.

It was not the hypocrisy alone that caused the Pharisees to be imbalanced. This may sound odd, but it is possible to be a student of the text and be as deliriously lost as the Pharisees were. The problem is that they could not see Jesus in the text (John 5.39). If they could have seen Jesus, they would have had a love for the Word, coupled with a deep love for people. This is true because they would see Jesus, who came to draw people to Himself, who came not for the whole but for the sick (Luke 5.31). So, again, if my preaching does not have a Christological center, I am missing the point of the text—every text—no matter how good a student I am. Each text points to Christ, and thus each text is preached with a compassion for those whom Christ came to save.

This is what is meant by preaching that is surrendered to the audience. It is preaching that reflects the compassion and learned skill of understanding where people are because this is who we are. John Bunyan relayed this autobiographical word about his compassion for people:

> In my preaching of the Word, I took special notice of the fact that the Lord had led me to begin where his Word begins—with sinners; that is, to condemn all flesh and to show

and allege that, because of sin, the curse of God by the law belongs to and lays hold of all people as they come into the world. . . . Indeed I have been to them as one sent from the dead; I went in chains myself to preach to those in chains.[4]

Inherent in our call as Christians is that we learn to see in the dark—to go as one in chains to those in bondage. It is an expression of our regeneration that should be magnified by the preacher who feels the double weight of being a brother's keeper and a shepherd. This shepherding, of course, was modeled by our Lord. James Stewart said it precisely:

> But while the basic message thus remains constant and invariable, our presentation of it must take account of, and be largely conditioned by, the actual world on which our eyes look out to-day. The gospel is not for an age, but for all time: yet it is precisely the particular age—this history's hour and none other—to which we are commissioned by God to speak. It is against the backdrop of the contemporary situation that we have to reinterpret the gospel once for all delivered to the saints; and it is within the framework of current hopes and fears that we have to show the commanding relevance of Jesus.[5]

THE INCARNATE MODEL

Think of communication as a borrowed art. In Genesis 1:26 God said, "Let Us make man in Our image, according to Our likeness." This verse has profound theological implications, primarily because we understand that before we were ever created, God self-existed as three in one.[6] The Father, the Son, and the Holy Spirit melded in

4. John Bunyan, *Grace Abounding to the Chief of Sinners* (Auburn, MA: Evangelical Press, 2000), 133.

5. Stewart, *Heralds of God*, 11.

6. For a discussion of traditional and other views of the plurality found in Genesis 1:26, see C. F. Keil and F. Delitzch, *Commentary on the Old Testament* (Grand Rapids: Eerdmans,

perfect union to create one who would reflect God's image. In each man and woman is the created reflection of the Father, the Son, and the Holy Spirit. For the purpose of this discussion, it is necessary to see in this text only that God communicated within Himself: the Father to the Son, the Son to the Spirit, the Spirit to the Father. Before one syllable was ever pronounced with human tongue, before there was any disparity in languages, God communicated. So this text is also important for the fact that it is the first recorded act of communication between individuals. Since God existed in perfection, we can safely conclude that before imperfect human communication took place, perfect divine communication took place. Communication is a borrowed art. It is a mortal reflection of what took place within immortality, a temporal expression of what existed in eternity past.

The seminal expression of this perfect communication was the incarnation of Christ. The Incarnation also took place in eternity past since Christ was crucified before the foundation of the world (cf. Eph. 1:3–6; Rev. 13:8). The effect was that while we were still in a sinful state, Christ died for us (Rom. 5:8). Why could one argue that this was the perfect communication? The answer is simple: the Incarnation was the perfect communication because it perfectly expressed God.

While God is a perfect communicator, we fail miserably. We stutter and stammer. We have to repeat ourselves. On our best days, we are precise, at least as precise as we can be. But that is just the problem; we are as precise as *we* can be. Our communication is frustratingly limited. The preacher, then, is doubly frustrated. He grapples with eternal truths, renames them, and then puts them out there, hoping that those in the dark will get a glimpse of what is in the light. The best sermons are still human constructions, unable to fully express the mysteries of God. And yet, this weak human communication is responsible for projecting the perfect Incarnation into new light. The Incarnation is the perfect form of communication because Jesus *was*

1975), 1:62; or see Gordon J. Wenham, *Genesis 1–15*, Word Biblical Commentary (Waco, TX: Word, 1987), 1:27–28.

the perfect expression of what the Father wanted to say. "He is the radiance of His glory and the *exact representation* of His nature" (Heb. 1:3, emphasis added). There is nothing the Father wanted to express that Jesus did not. Before He ever opened His mouth, He was exactly what the Father wanted to say. He was perfect communication. While this is interesting, it is hardly the fascinating part.

The fascinating aspect of Christ's incarnation as perfect communication is that He communicated perfectly in an imperfect world, surrounded by imperfect people, and wrapped in dying flesh. Jesus lived in a world where people maligned, hated, and destroyed what was good, while they relished and praised evil. He was in an environment where things died and stank. The vile was common, the beautiful was rare, and the perfect nonexistent. This is why the words of Jesus are so stark. They jut out as a blinding light against the blazing darkness in which He came. So what does this perfect communication mean to us as preachers?

First, we are mindful that our imperfect communication is a reflection of this perfect communication. Thus the pains taken to sharpen communication are themselves an appreciation for Godlike, perfect communication. Since the art is borrowed, it bodes well for our efforts when they give credence to the Creator, the original Communicator. Second, we will never communicate in a perfect environment, nor were we intended to.

It is tempting to think that given the right personal circumstances and the right environment for preaching, one could preach the perfect sermon. Jesus preached from a boat, Paul on a Greek hillside, Peter in the temple courtyard, Savonarola in an Italian piazza, and Whitefield in a farm pasture. The point is that Jesus did His best work in bad situations. The moment did not create spiritual power; rather spiritual power created the moment.

Finally, we learn from the Incarnation that perfect communication has as its end the salvation of sinners. Perfect communication sees in the dark for the purpose of illustrating to others what is in the light. This was Jesus' whole point! What more could be our objective? We who live in the light must learn to squint. We are seeing in the dark so that others will not have to. This is the profound power of the Incarnation and our impetus and model to surrender our communication for those who will hear. Our reasons, then, for this surrender to the listener are twofold. First, it is the nature of the call of Christians that we love others, especially the lost, more than ourselves. Second, our communication should strive to be a reflection of the perfect communication that exists only in God. The perfect expression of that perfect communication and the one closest to us is the Incarnation, through which we learn that communication does not take place in a perfect context and that real communication is where people live. Shepherds smell like sheep, and surrendered communicators have a "feel" for people who are in the dark. How is this surrender expressed in preaching? What follows is a word on Fénelon's take on the subject, followed by a practical working out of surrender to the audience.

FÉNELON'S UNDERSTANDING OF SURRENDER TO THE AUDIENCE

Early in the *Dialogues*, the character A, a wise sage who represents Fénelon's view of rhetoric, challenges the young naive C with a reduction of eloquence into three categories. He says,

> Eloquence, if I do not fool myself, can be taken as three things: 1.) as the art of persuading men of the truth and making them better; 2.) as a neutral art which the mischievous as well as the good can make use of, and which enforce falsehood and injustice no less than justice and truth; 3.) and lastly, as an art which selfish men can use in order to give pleasure, to acquire a reputation, and to make their fortune.[7]

Fénelon (who at this point is speaking only of oratory in general—his application to preaching, however, is obvious) is trying to show

---

7. Fénelon, *Dialogues on Eloquence*, 65.

three applications of oratory. The purpose of this reduction to three is to show the character C what true preaching is.

The first way to understand preaching is as an art that persuades people toward truth and results in making them better. Under this theory, preaching can have only one aim, namely, to change lives through the explanation of truth. Since the truth is found in the Scripture, this preaching is simply the art of life change through the expository teaching of Scripture.

The second way of looking at eloquent preaching is as a neutral art that can be used for either good or bad. Some can use preaching as a means of good, but others can be eloquent and use preaching for evil, selfish ends. In this view, eloquent communication can serve good or bad ends.

Finally, eloquent preaching can be used as a means toward a selfish end. Thus, the preacher can hone his craft for the sake of a higher salary, greater reputation, or the mere pleasure of the audience. This preacher may use the Scripture to make a point. He may even use the tools of exposition to convey that he has studied and is prepared. The difference here is the aim, the objective. In his heart he is ruled by what every preacher has to fight—the use of the pulpit for selfish objectives. His logic is that the better preachers get the bigger salaries, so he commits his life to entertaining his way to success.

All of the above definitions are used to describe preaching. We would have to be honest enough to say that as preachers, we have viewed preaching, and even preached, from all of these perspectives. The last two definitions describe temptations inherent in the call. It is the beast that must be killed each time we preach. Now, since someone can hear a sermon and not be quite sure of the aim, motivation, or heart of the preacher, one might say that all three of these preaching theories are equal. After all, we reason, each approach has the same results. People respond as well to one with the right motivation as to one with the wrong motivation. In fact, when the preacher is not so concerned about getting some truth across, it gives him more freedom to get even a better response from the audience. However, an examination of each application will illustrate that while all three approaches may induce an emotional response, only one can be considered eloquent.

The first view obviously is the argument for text-driven preaching and is the perspective that Fénelon is trying to propose. The second view—that preaching is a neutral art—could not be true eloquence, since it allows for the art to be used for evil as well as good. True biblical preaching would never, under anyone's definition, be considered eloquent if it were used to persuade one toward evil. Preaching, then, cannot be neutral. Eloquent preaching cannot be both good and bad. If preaching persuades one toward falsehood, toward that which is harmful, then it is bad and in no way could be considered eloquent. The final approach to preaching, that of serving personal interest, is a little more challenging for the young naive in the *Dialogues* to grasp. The practical question of the third theory is "If a preacher is entertaining and motivating, but his aim is to earn money and reputation, what is the harm? Is not the net effect of people being inspired and moved the same as for the one who has a pure motivation?" A little historical context would be appropriate here.

Fénelon leans heavily on the Greek masters of rhetoric. In ancient Greece some orators were little more than speech-making hired guns. They would leave their personal beliefs aside and, for a good fee, would speak on any topic whatsoever. They would argue a case before the government, make a public speech, or argue a case in court. The idea was that their skill won them reputation, their reputation won them opportunities to perform, and these opportunities provided a nice income. Come forward about 1,200 years to seventeenth-century France, where Fénelon sees the same oratorical practice alive in his time. The reputation-seeking aim of the orators was not so overt, yet it was nevertheless real. There were those in the clergy who were good preachers, and their objective was fame and fortune; that is, a good reputation and a good living.

Obviously there are many blessings that come from being faithful to God, and sometimes those blessings come in the form of tangible, material things. This often follows faithfulness to God's Word and a lot of hard work. The point is not that the provision for the minister is bad. The point is that a hunger for them should not precede the preaching ministry. Fénelon is dealing with what happens before the sermon is preached, namely, the motivation for crafting and shaping the sermon.

It is an interesting observation that when one is faithful to preach Scripture, God often will add what the preacher did not expect, blessings on which he did not count. Since this is true, it may be easy for one on the outside to view material blessings as the motivation for a preacher, when this may not be the motivation at all. The point does not need to be belabored. It is enough to know that God does bless us. The problem is when people interpret these blessings as the objective of the preacher or, conversely, when the preacher aims for these things as the motivation of his preaching. The preacher who has temporal gain as his objective cannot see in the dark, for his preaching serves his goals and not the needs of the congregation. This brings us back to the question, "What is wrong with preaching that inspires and entertains, even if the preacher is motivated by reputation and money?" The following section will deviate slightly from the issue of preaching in order to eventually answer this question.

PERSUASION, ART, AND ENTERTAINMENT

Why should a preacher not seek to be entertaining above all else? It's simple really. Christ was motivated by love for people, and, as we have established, it is the nature of the call to be selfless as Christ was selfless in the Incarnation. Christ was not trying to please the audience or gain a reputation. However, presently Fénelon is not arguing as a Christian per se but from logic that is supported by Scripture. The reason the third approach is bad is that art, as mentioned in the second chapter, cannot exist in a vacuum of persuasion. All art, whether music, dance, cinema, theatre, or fine arts, is on some level persuasive. This is why parents are rightly concerned with the art to which their children are exposed. Amusement that is corrupt can be more damaging than a corrupt schoolteacher. The art (music, drama, dance) is simply a more powerful and entertaining medium, thus it wields as much or more influence than a teacher. Rarely does a student come home from school wearing the fashion of his humanities teacher, but many a parent has been puzzled over an adolescent interpretation of fashion generated by popular culture. Amusement does not just amuse; it persuades. Art moves the participant from one opinion to another. Entertainment will always persuade on some level. One might argue that this is exactly why preachers must be entertaining. If preaching is an art, and art persuades, then let the preachers be entertaining since they can then persuade toward ultimate truth! Let church be fun above all else, since that will move people toward the truth they should embrace. Since this approach is obviously a trend in the church, some thoughts will be offered here using Fénelon as our guide.

Fénelon believed it was important to *distinguish between what is pleasing and what is entertaining.* A "good" singer is more pleasing to the ear than one who is not skilled as a singer. This does not mean that her objective is entertainment alone. She may be aiming to please God with a pure heart. The fact that she has good vocal quality and is pleasing to the ear facilitates the worship of God. I often have heard people dismiss quality worship as "mere entertainment," seemingly because it was good. This is piety in the worst form. The logic is that all pleasure in art is entertainment and all entertainment is bad; therefore, if I felt pleasure as I listened to the music, it must be bad. The worst part of this logic is that it naively discriminates between the secular and the sacred. It is almost a Gnostic approach that says what is material is bad and what is spiritual and invisible is good. All of God's creation was made for mankind's enjoyment. God wants us to enjoy Him. He delights in those who delight in Him. Beautiful art can help us appreciate the glory of God that He has displayed toward us. Thus Fénelon wisely distinguished between pleasure aimed toward instruction and pleasure whose end was pleasure alone. The former serves the objective of teaching; the latter serves only self. He wrote,

> The good man seeks to please only that he may urge justice and the other virtues by making them attractive. He who seeks his own interest, his reputation, his fortune, dreams of pleasing only that he may gain the bow and esteem of men able to satisfy his greed or his ambition.[8]

Pleasure is a part of our worship, and it is the preacher's tool for instruction. However, there are three inherent dangers when art is used to express the beauty of God; the first deals with the art itself, and the second and third with the artist.

First, there is the danger *that pleasing art can become the objective of preaching, not a means of instruction.* If art is used to express worship to God, then the value of the worship can be reduced to the presentation of the art itself. In this scenario, the song, the sermon, or the art is not evaluated by the integrity of the presenter, the theological integrity of the song, or its appropriateness to the moment. Rather, the art is evaluated by its entertainment value, which is often measured by its immediate effect on the audience. It could be that a pulsating desire for entertainment, or the innocent desire of a well-meaning preacher, has welcomed entertainment into the church with little discretion. With all respect given to beauty that brings pleasure, we must be cautious lest every form of communication be judged by entertainment criteria. This could leave little room for intercession or the serious truths of Scripture that need explanation from the pulpit and celebration from the pew. One might argue that contemporary people simply want a quality presentation. This, of course, is not bad in itself and in fact may push a preacher and a church to be more excellent, more refined.

However, imbedded in the desire for refinement is a subtle but real temptation, namely, that *while positive virtues bring refinement,*

---

8. Ibid., 62.

152 Dying to Preach

refinement left unchecked degenerates little by little.[9] The Greeks were the most refined of all ancient civilizations. But when the refined taste became their objective, they became effeminate, immoral, and lax. If not guarded against, refinement leads to mere pleasure seeking, which leads to a pure hedonism. This is certainly where our culture is, and it is in this culture that we preach. This may seem like an obscure place to make this point, but its application to preaching is important. Our culture is constantly fine-tuning its taste and appreciation for certain types of art. The trend is reminiscent of pagan cultures that followed hedonism. If the focus of our sermons is the art of preaching itself, then we have trained our people to watch for an art above and beyond the truth that is presented. The method of preaching, as noted in chapter 2, becomes the message itself. Thus, the objective of communicating truth is lost because the method is giving mixed signals. The pursuit of art alone is discordant with the message to focus on Christ alone. I am aware that I am dealing with subtleties that not all will appreciate. It is worth taking the risk. The sermon must be so focused on the person of Christ, so that while the art of the well-crafted sermon is pleasing, the pleasure serves only to facilitate the truth, and not merely to develop an appetite for entertaining speeches.

If there is an appetite for entertaining speeches alone, then a third problem surfaces. *If the sermon is evaluated by its entertainment quality alone, then the preacher himself must be judged on his ability to be entertaining.* Fénelon believed that the preacher should teach, paint the message clearly, and then persuade people of the truth. When this is done well, it is provocative. A good sermon is pleasing to listen to because of the pains taken to teach, paint, and persuade, even when the message of the Scripture is difficult to swallow. Judging by the criteria of entertainment, Jesus was not an entertaining communicator. In fact, excepting the miracles, His crowds got smaller. This also could be said for Paul, who did not think of himself as a profound communicator. Jonathan Edwards is famous as the last great Puritan thinker, the greatest American theologian of his time, and a phenomenal preacher. His delivery, however, was less than entertaining, as he was known to read his sermons early in his life.[10] The presence of the Holy Spirit was more profound than the need for entertainment, however, and his sermons sparked the Second Great Awakening in America. On the other hand, George Whitefield has been called the "Divine Dramatist."[11] His passionate oratory was known as part theater and part Scripture. Yet, he too was greatly used of God. It was pleasing art that was tempered by a pure ambition. The point is that all preachers should strive to be pleasing, but the entertainment value of the sermon does not carry the message. The sermons are weighed by their faithfulness to the text, resulting in long-term effects on people.

CONCLUSION

The following conversation in the *Dialogues*, speaking of orators, sums it up precisely:

> They speak to persuade—that is what they always do. They speak also to please—that is merely what they too often do. But when they seek to please, they have another more distant aim, which is nevertheless the principal one. The good man seeks to please only that he may urge justice and other virtues by making them attractive. He who seeks his own interest, his reputation, his fortune, dreams of pleasing only that he may gain the bow and esteem of men able to satisfy his greed or his ambition. Thus, even his case can be reduced like that of the good man to persuasion as the single aim which a speaker has; for the self-interested man wishes to

---

10. Toby Easley documents that Edwards moved away from manuscript preaching later in his ministry, shaking the caricature of a stayed presentation often associated with his preaching. Easley suggests this was due to the influence of Whitefield. See "Jonathan Edwards: Extemporaneous or Manuscript Preacher?" presented to Evangelical Theological Society, Southwest Region, Fort Worth, TX, March 23, 2007.

11. Harry S. Stout, *The Divine Dramatist: George Whitefield and the Rise of Modern Evangelicalism* (Grand Rapids: Eerdmans, 1991).

please in order to flatter, and he flatters in order to inculcate that which suits his interest.[12]

Fénelon observed a dichotomy between those who were self-seeking and those who strove to serve God and others in their preaching. While we know that blessings follow those who serve God, we must confess that the lives of preachers in third-world nations prove that obedience is not always rewarded with popularity, praise, or material abundance. According to Fénelon, one must choose between preaching for others or for self—there is no middle ground. Great preaching must serve the purposes of eloquence: to teach, to portray, and to persuade. The question remains as to what exactly he meant by this definition of eloquence and why it is an important goal to aim for in communication.

12. Fénelon, *Dialogues on Eloquence*, 65.

[9]

Surrendered to the Task of Great Preaching

When I finished this chapter, which encourages us to become proficient at the task of preaching, a friend of mine read the chapter and pointed out that it was suspiciously lacking in Scripture. Then, after rereading it, I was forced to ask this interesting, and perhaps obvious, question: Is it *biblical* to want to preach good sermons? Is there something inherently wrong in this ambition? Is it pure narcissistic hubris to grow in the proficiency of a task that is used of God to accomplish *His* ends?

Of course we could scramble for verses that suggest all things should be done for God's glory (cf. 1 Cor. 10:31). And there are texts that suggest that preaching especially should be done with excellence:

> Whoever speaks, *is to do so* as one who is speaking the utterances of God; whoever serves *is to do so* as one who is serving by the strength which God supplies; so that in all things God may be glorified through Jesus Christ, to whom belongs the glory and dominion forever and ever. Amen. (1 Peter 4:11)

> All Scripture is inspired by God and profitable for teaching, for reproof, for correction, for training in righteousness; so that the man of God may be adequate, equipped for every good work. (2 Tim. 3:16–17)

While these texts should not be underestimated, they do not tell me why I should try to do better at, expend energy for, something in which God is going to bring the results. Isn't better preaching simply a means to the end of self-aggrandizement? Isn't the history of the church filled with examples of God blessing average preaching, as well as bad preaching? The answer is not really.

Of course God does not need us. Of course He uses the weak to confound the wise (1 Cor. 1:26–31). This is His glory. However, the history of the church points to God using men who were proficient in their task. From Augustine to Savonarola, to Spurgeon, to Whitefield, to Wesley, to Edwards, to Manton, to Massillon, and many, many others who were defined by the fact that they were, to say it crassly, *good*. This is not intended to discourage those who are not naturally gifted. Rather it is intended to motivate the bulk of us who have been entrusted with average gifts. *We must become better in our preaching because God uses good preaching.* With all the liabilities we have mentioned, with all of the red flags about style over substance, with all the warnings about a self-centered pulpit, we must commit ourselves to becoming good preachers. So with eight chapters of warning against letting the *good* of decent preaching rob people of the *best* of seeing Christ in the text, let me stop and scream, "Strive for good preaching!"

If you were to go to the archives of Yale University, you would find the original manuscript of Jonathan Edwards's sermon "Sinners in the Hands of an Angry God." Perhaps it is the most famous sermon in American history. It is written out in longhand, in roughly twenty-four small pages. The image that is often perceived of Edwards is that he is holding these pages inches from his nose as he reads the manuscript. This is a part of our collective understanding of Edwards and the First Great Awakening.

However, there is something interesting about that manuscript. If you were to look in the back, you will see two pages that are a sketch of the whole outline. It seems that, under the influence of the preaching of Whitefield, Edwards was convicted of the power of extemporaneous preaching and shifted his sermon delivery. No longer did he use the manuscript, but rather he made the conscious decision to shift away from notes. I am not sure that there is a better illustration of humility in the history of preaching. The man who would preach what is later known as the best sermon in American history wanted to improve his preaching!

I use this illustration because I fear that our collective perception of the stilted delivery of Edwards has framed for us a license to be weak in our sermon delivery and "let God take care of the rest." "After all," we muse, "should we think of being better than Edwards?" Please remember, Edwards was not satisfied with the preaching of Edwards. We should not be satisfied with our preaching either.[1]

What is our motivation to move forward with relentless, aggressive tenacity toward becoming effective preachers? The answer—the only one that gives me a modicum of satisfaction—is the cross. Christ expended everything on the cross, because leaving anything undone would not have accomplished God's will. What would it be like to look back at a preached sermon and say that it is finished; that in every way possible, I completed the work that God sent me to do? The completed work of Christ cannot be duplicated. It is unique. We are not perfect. However, should not the completed work of Christ be my motivation not to give up on a sermon till it is finished and effective? This just makes sense: a message of completion from a sermon that is complete, a message of compassion from a messenger so compassionate that he is willing to die just so that the message will be effectively delivered. Can a message of completion be mediated from a half-baked sermon?

---

1. Regarding this two-page version of "Sinners," historian Harry Stout wrote, "The outline would compel him to preach extemporaneously and connect personally with his listeners. . . . For all the attention paid to 'Sinners,' no one has appreciated the significance of this fragment version. It confirms the novelty of the sermon, not only on the level of content and rhetoric in print, but of its extemporaneous abbreviation. Assuming that Edwards delivered this sermon on more than two occasions, we can see this two-page fragment text as the real 'Sinners' sermon, the highly portable and powerful cue card allowing multiple deliveries—and unprecedented terror. Contained in these two pages was rhetorical dynamite." Harry S. Stout, "Edwards and Revival," in *Understanding Jonathan Edwards: An Introduction to America's Theologian*, ed. Gerald R. McDermott (New York: Oxford, 2009).

Of course God can use a bad sermon as well as a good sermon. Praise Him for the fact that He works in spite of my weakness! Praise Him that He even does great things with poor sermons just to teach me that this is His work, not mine! Praise Him for redeeming stinking sermons. Praise Him for touching hearts when my efforts are so wildly outside the strike zone. However, the logic of the cruciform life is that if there is a Christian life, it *is* a crucified life, wholly given over to God. So if there is proclamation, it *is* done with surrendered excellence to His glory. To be a Christian by definition *is* to live a cross-centered life. To preach *is* to preach in a surrendered way. To preach, by very definition, is to completely die so that others might live. To communicate the gospel is to work at the craft of communication. To do otherwise is to be completely inconsistent with the Christian message. Bad preaching is not Christian. So let's think about the work of preaching well.

OF BOREDOM AND PREACHING

Have you ever heard a boring sermon? Maybe the preacher taught well, had a good exposition of Scripture, and even illustrated the text well. He was just boring. He may have yelled louder to try to compensate for the monotony, but to no avail. It is reminiscent of the old joke about the preacher who wrote in the margin of his notes, "Weak point. Talk louder here." If great preaching is anything, it is the ability to be captivating—to know how to "hold" an audience. Fénelon referred to great preaching as that which was "eloquent." That word is lost on us. Today we would rather hear a communicator than an orator. So what is it that Fénelon meant by eloquence, and why is it important?

It may seem illogical to place the chapter on eloquence at the end of the book. However, all of these surrenders are necessary before one can become an effective preacher. The effective, surrendered preacher has released himself in abandonment to the one who gave him his voice to begin with and is therefore willing to die to himself so that others might live through the Word. The surrendered communicator is surrendered to the text in that he defers to Scripture above all else. The surrendered communicator also is surrendered to the audience. This is the communicator who has learned to see in the dark, taking the light to those who cannot see. Once these qualities are in place, the communicator is free to be eloquent. The reverse, however, is not true. By this I mean that preaching outside of these qualities—a death to self, a surrender to the text, a surrender to the audience—cannot be eloquent. Why? Precisely because if eloquent preaching is defined outside of preaching that is committed to God, the text, and to others, then eloquence will have to be defined in strange ways.

For example, if preaching is defined as eloquent, and yet it is not surrendered to God, this eloquent preaching is allowed to draw attention to someone other than God. It is self-seeking. It is self-service. Preaching cannot serve God and the preacher's selfish ends. Preaching that sounds flowery, authentic, relational, or whatever but does not have as its aim to please God and is not birthed from a man completely surrendered to God must be defined as great words without substance. Eloquence has lost its meaning. True eloquence comes from surrender to God. This is the prerequisite. This is the essential. Without this foundation, preaching is built on human reasoning and will not pass the ultimate test of long-term results. This also is the purpose of this book, namely, to be an apologetic for text-driven preaching, which has in mind to explain the text, which will explain Christ, who will explain God. This explanation of the text assumes that the text is from God; therefore the preacher remains under the text. With this foundation laid, this chapter will deal with the final surrender, the surrender to the challenging work of excellent preaching itself.

RECOVERING "ELOQUENCE"

There are many adjectives that one could use for good preaching: excellent, great, effective, powerful, far-reaching, beautiful, relevant, or persuasive. The word Fénelon used, *eloquence,* is outdated. The word brings to mind a golden age of preaching and the image of the gifted orator who alliterates and pontificates, all the while cognizant of the power of his words over the congregation. The audience sits spellbound. They have never heard such words in such a way. The brilliance of the oratory sweeps them away in a moment of sheer spiritual translation. They are lost in his powerful words and are highly suggestible since they are under the power of such communication. The truth is that this image is far from the reality that most preachers experience. In fact, I would argue that few preachers today even aim for this definition of "eloquence." The reason is simple.

Today there is a profound suspicion of people who sound like preachers. Preachers are among the most highly educated people in the community but often are the least respected. While the preacher has poured passion and energy into his calling, he enters the work with one strike against him, namely, that he is in fact a preacher. There is little confidence in him and even less respect. In fact, things reminiscent of good preaching, the booming voice and the flowery words, often "paint" the preacher in such a way that they contribute to the stereotype and ironically project the very image from which the preacher would like to escape. Preachers have reacted to this cultural reality primarily in one of two ways.[2]

The first reaction is to stay within the tradition. Some have feared that to give up the established model of preaching—in essence, heavy alliteration and the traditional model of rhetorical outline—is to give up the spirit of preaching. Often those who grieve over the decline in recognition of the authority of God's Word will gravitate to an approach that is reminiscent of a day when people did recognize the authority of the Word. Thus the means of communicating the authority of the Word is forever tied to the method of communicating the Word. To separate the two is to jeopardize one or the other.

The second reaction is to avoid anything that sounds like a preacher at all. This more contemporary approach will almost apologize for

2. The following models put forth here intentionally paint with very broad brushstrokes for the purpose of presenting a picture of effective preaching. Many preachers, of course, are a mix of these two approaches, using the best of both effectively.

preaching. The dress, demeanor, mannerisms, and choice of words say, "Hey, I am just a pilgrim trying to figure this out. Here are a few things I have learned." Relevance is the goal; therefore the approach is a conversation, not a presentation. Personal pronouns like *you* have been replaced by *we* to illustrate a collective sense of the journey the group is taking together. It is most likely that for those taking this approach, the idea of recovering eloquence seems neither likely nor desirable. Flowery preaching may not be dead, but there is someone in a black-and-white striped shirt standing over it counting, and the count is already up to eight.

For these reasons, I thought to abandon the word *eloquence* altogether. However, there is no word that communicates Fénelon's thought exactly. Let me clarify the use of this word *eloquence*. Like Fénelon I am not arguing for flowery preaching. Today adding pretty sounding words to your sermon may be highly *ineffective* communication. By eloquence *I mean simply that which is effective in drawing people into the text.* Do people hear the text clearly and understand it? Are they persuaded to do what it says? This is eloquence.

Perhaps the "means" of preaching has received more attention than necessary. There are those who preach in a way reminiscent of the good old days of preaching, but they are not saying what the text says, illustrating it, and then persuading people to do it. In other words, their faithfulness is to a method more than to the idea of communication or to faithfulness to the text. This is not eloquence. Conversely, there are those whose aim is not sounding like a preacher. However, they have not said what the text says, illustrated it, or persuaded people to follow its precepts. This is faithfulness to an ideology of relevance in ministry, but not faithfulness to Scripture.

A thousand times I would repeat the words of chapter 3: style is not unimportant, but style is not ultimate. It's the last question, not the first. The Scripture is ultimate, therefore I have died to the idea of using the pulpit as a place to manage my reputation. The sheep *must hear the Word clearly, have it illustrated effectively, and then be persuaded to do what it says.* This is eloquence as defined by Fénelon:

to teach, to portray, and to persuade.[3] Therefore, a commitment to eloquence is a commitment to grow in the task of the exposition of the Word.

To this point we have argued for the exposition of the text and the surrender that this demands from the preacher to the text itself, to God, and to others. The primary discussion has been the "why" of preaching. As we move to a discussion of Fénelon's understanding of eloquence, it will become necessary to deal slightly with the "what" and "how." How does one teach a text, paint a text, and then persuade others to obedience to it?

THE TASK OF ELOQUENCE

The task of eloquence is to carry the meaning of the text to the hearer in a way that is clear and compelling and persuades them to action.

What makes a preacher compelling? What about the presentation of the sermon draws one into the message, provokes interest in the subject, retains interest, and persuades the listener to follow the precepts of the Scripture? Is it plausible that one could have all the qualities of a surrendered communicator and still be a very boring preacher? In fact, often the chief criticism of text-driven preaching is that it is not compelling; it is not interesting because it is simply not where people live. While it is plausible that there is a difference between one who has commitment to the task and a compelling voice that draws the listener into the text, a surrendered communicator is never boring. Why? The answer is that Scripture itself is compelling, provocative, interesting, and fascinating. There is mystery, intrigue, and suspense. The questions posed by Scripture deal with issues vital to one's existence and therefore are engaging at every level. It takes a real effort to make the Scriptures seem boring. Exposition does not make the Scripture boring; preachers make the Scripture boring. We

---

3. Fénelon's exact words are translated "to prove, to portray, and to strike." Howell argues that these are an adaptation of Cicero's theory of the three means of persuasion. See Francois Fénelon, *Dialogues on Eloquence* (Princeton, NJ: Princeton University Press, 1951), 92n. 38.

veil the thrill of the text with language that does not move, shake, and bite.

There are two reasons we preachers seem to make the Scripture boring. First, *boredom* is an elastic term based on culture and personality. What might be a compelling sermon in the Northeast may be a sleeper in the West. And it goes without saying that some personalities are simply more compelling than others. The second, more prominent reason a sermon is boring is that there is surrender to the text and yet no surrender to the audience. A preacher who is completely surrendered to the text yet not surrendered to the audience will be a lecturer who is not concerned with the element of connection that needs to be present with an audience. He makes a complete effort to insure that what is said about the text is correct, but he doesn't go the "second mile" of making sure what is said communicates. The surrendered communicator goes the second mile.

I often have thought that some of the best words and phrases in the English language, the most poetic and descriptive, have potential to be poor communication. While the use of beautiful language from the pulpit may lift the spirits and educate the audience, there is the danger that people simply will not understand what is said. If the pretty words do not get the message across, then, ironically, the nice words do not communicate. When the expositor's spirit is surrendered to the audience, this may translate to fewer of our favorite phrases and more digging to find what will really "speak" to the audience.

This raises the issue of the use of theological terms. It may be wise not to introduce theological terms into the pulpit, unless those words can be defined and are essential to theological understanding. When speaking of the atonement, the word *propitiation* carries a meaning that no other word exactly carries. The words *substitution, in our place,* and *in our stead* don't say exactly what *propitiation* says. The idea, of course, is that Jesus satisfied the wrath of God as our substitute. He took our hell. Since the word is unique in that its presence carries a theological doctrine that no other word does, and the preacher understands it well enough to define it, its use and definition would be plausible in a sermon. The point is to determine the importance of the word. Can you define it and does it carry a theological thought unique to its usage? If so, it will be worth the effort to use and explain the word. The goal is effective communication, not sounding bright and educated. (Nor of course is the goal to sound uneducated.)

By the way, there are two types of boring sermons. The first is emotionally boring. This is the sermon that is so void of engagement that it puts people to sleep. Wanting to avoid this, perhaps we have opted for the second type—the intellectually boring sermon. This is the sermon that is very engaging, funny, interesting, and compelling. However, the sermon is so oriented toward felt needs that the listener is never challenged to think deeply about God. My suspicion is that the church loses college students because their pastors don't make them think. Maybe they make them laugh and cry, but not think. So while the sermon engages the emotions, it bores the mind.

Communication, then, is focused. It is precise. A great preacher will be notable for what he does not say, as much as for what he says. This is the discipline of the surrendered communicator. The task of eloquence is to carry the meaning of the text to the hearer in a way that is clear, compelling, and leads them to action.

The remainder of this chapter will focus on the three goals of the surrendered communicator. These are the elements that Fénelon thought were essential to eloquent communication: teaching, portraying, and persuading.

Teaching

What is the greatest compliment that could be paid to a preacher—"Great style," "You really made me laugh!" or perhaps, "I really felt what you were saying"? These phrases indicate that at least the sermon was not emotionally boring. They may even indicate that the preacher has a gift for connecting with an audience. However, the surrendered communicator is convinced that the power of the message is the power of Scripture. Therefore, the most help the sermon can be to anyone is when the sermon clearly explains Scripture. Perhaps the greatest compliment a preacher could be paid is, "Now I understand what the Scripture means!" At this point the listener has confidence that the preacher has explained Scripture. Can't the listeners get the same from a lecture? Absolutely not. The reason is simple. Scripture was not written for intellectual stimulation alone. It was written to help the people understand and follow God. If the listeners do not see the word pictures the preacher is painting, if they are not compelled to do what the Scripture says, then they do not understand. Understanding is a blend of hearing and obedience. In other words, meaning comes from a heart that is compelled to obey. What distinguishes the surrendered communicator from a lecturer is the compelling way in which the listener is called to action.

Scriptural ignorance in the pew is perhaps the most compelling motivation for preaching that is surrendered to the text. Even if we do not consider ourselves great "teachers," a preacher who is wholly committed to the text of Scripture will always teach. Why is this? The preacher who has committed himself wholly to the study of Scripture will come to it with a resounding sense that this is God's Word to him. The joy of discovering truth in God's Word will change the man as he studies, and the changed heart will be reflected from the pulpit. This is the model of transformational preaching: a powerful text, a changed heart, and a passionate explanation of the text from someone who is now living proof of its power. That passion will move the explanation of the text from a dry lecture to a vibrant display of all the beauty and power that is in the passage. Thus, a surrendered communicator will not only say what the text says in a compelling way but also will paint and portray the text in a way that gives an accurate picture of its meaning.[4]

PORTRAYING

Fénelon believed that the second task of the orator is to portray, or paint, his subject. By this he meant that it simply is not enough to say

---

4. Since chapter 7, "Surrendered to the Text," dealt primarily with the teaching function of the preacher from Scripture, we will leave the discussion of the teaching function with these words alone.

what the text is saying; the speaker must say it in such a way that it draws the listener to attention. He wrote,

> To portray is not only to describe things but to represent their surrounding features in so lively and so concrete a way that the listener imagines himself almost seeing them.[5]

Thus to portray is to re-present something. It is to use words to paint pictures. When this is done effectively, one will not even be aware it is taking place. No one will leave thinking the preacher really painted with his words. The artist is hidden behind the art. The beauty of what is seen with the mind's eye is so pronounced that one hardly notices the one doing the portraying of what is seen. In this moment Fénelon observes that *le poete disparoit,* the poet disappears. This is portraiture. It is what an artist does on a canvas when he paints a picture that reflects his craftsmanship, but not him directly. Fénelon writes,

> The poet disappears. You see nothing but that which he makes visible; you hear nothing but those whom he makes speak. There one sees the power of imitation and portraiture! Hence it comes about that the painter and the poet have so close a connection: the one paints for the eyes, the other for the ears. Both the one and the other assume the duty of carrying objects over into the imagination of men.[6]

This is what the preacher and the painter have in common.

Fénelon felt so strongly about the use of the words to enforce the message that he believed no one could be eloquent without being a poet. By poetry he did not mean words written in verse. Rather he meant a lively use of words to describe what normally would be boring and static. Without this, he argued, everything would be dull and lifeless.

---

5. Fénelon, *Dialogues on Eloquence,* 73.
6. Ibid.

Probably all would agree on the power of words to translate meaning in a picturesque way, but there are some natural objections to using words in such a way. The first objection is one already mentioned, namely, that flowery words make one sound too much like, well, like a preacher. Let us distinguish between flowery words and words that paint. What we would call flowery words are words that are a means unto themselves. They merely serve to illustrate the vocabulary of the user and his affinity for pretty sounding words. Words that paint pictures serve the purpose of making the truth clearer, thus aiding in understanding.

In an interesting comparison to architecture, Fénelon compared flowery words to gothic architecture with all its gargoyles, intricate designs, and curvatures. He compared useful words that paint to classical Greco-Roman architecture with its straight and clean lines. In other words, the Greco-Roman architecture was beautiful in its own right, but form followed function; that is, everything had a purpose. Gothic structures, however, were excessively elaborate, with intricacies that were not structurally necessary to the building and did not flow naturally with the architecture. Matters of taste notwithstanding, his analogy works. Words either serve the preacher or the listener, and a "dead" preacher chooses the latter.

The second objection is that the use of beautiful words that paint do not sound real; they sound affected. However, it is wise to think of these words as contrast words. If a preacher uses a conversational tone in his approach, painting a word picture of the grotesque nature of Jonah's living conditions in the belly of the fish or of the beautiful majesty of Christ as portrayed in Revelation 19, this will be such a contrast to his normal pattern of speech that the congregation will be provoked. Their interest will be piqued.

A final objection is that being a wordsmith takes too much effort. To learn to describe an image or a situation in words that are compelling and interesting simply takes too much time. This is truer for some than for others. While some preachers are poetic on their feet, others have to put a great deal of thought into what words will graphically describe something. It may be tempting to forget the whole idea and just say what Scripture says. But remember, Jesus painted pictures with His words. The dozens of parables Jesus told indicate that some things are not caught in lectures alone. If there is truth that will not be caught unless it is painted for the hearers, then effective communication has not taken place until it is painted before them.

How does one who is not a natural word painter learn to paint with words? Take a tip from a popular board game Taboo. The game asks teams to guess the word a teammate is describing. The player giving the clues cannot use certain descriptive words that are taboo. Write out a story you want to tell, or a principle you want to communicate. After you write the story out, think of all the adjectives or verbs in the story as taboo. This will force you to retell the story in a way that is compelling and interesting. Let's return to an earlier example. Without portraiture one might say, "Jesus died on the cross to save us from our sins."

With those verbs taboo, we would be forced to be more creative:

> Jesus was brutally murdered on a cross to ensure that we would not face the punishment we had coming for all the crimes against God we gladly committed.

We said the same thing, but, oh, how the meaning changes. The truth of the matter is the second version is more theologically accurate since it more clearly gives the essence of what happened. I am convinced that the same is true with all theological axioms we tend to throw around. Phrases such as "God has a plan for you" and "All things work out for good" are so bland and open-ended they have lost their meaning to the point of inaccuracy. They are neither precise nor descriptive.

PERSUADING

Persuasion has taken a bad rap. In fact, one could argue that persuasion is out of vogue in the pulpit. Why is persuasion neglected in so many sermons? The uniform answer is that people are tired of being told what to do. Persuasion carries the heavy connotation of a sweaty evangelist strolling the aisles of the church, begging people to respond to the message. Before we get to what Fénelon had to say, let us address the common objection to using persuasion in the sermon.

It is true that some have been persuasive on a manipulative level and have done so for seemingly short-term results. No one would discount that. However, there is a more probable reason that preachers have left persuasion out of their messages. The reason is simple. To persuade is to call someone from one position to hold another position. For a preacher, this means calling people from one position to what he better be convinced is God's position on the subject. This implies two things. First, it implies that the persons listening to the sermon are wrong. There is something askew. While they know it to be true and the preacher knows it to be true, today it is considered an affront to their sensibilities to acknowledge this out loud. Second, it also implies that the preacher has the answer. He is right. "He is not so perfect, so where does he get off telling me what to do?" people reason.

The reason persuasion is out of vogue in the pew is that it flows against the stream of relativism to assume that people are out of step. Yet people are saying, "If I am truth to myself, why should I be persuaded to anything?" The reason persuasion is out of vogue in the pulpit is that preachers have started to believe this lie. Even in pulpits that tout the most conservative theology, there is an inherent trepidation to lead anyone to another position.

Dear preacher, as relational and culturally sensitive as we want to be, we are not one of the crowd. We are mouthpieces, prophets. The idea of a clerical buddy was lost on Paul, Peter, Titus, and Timothy. There is a prophetic edge to our message. If we run from or do not acknowledge that prophetic voice, it does not go away. God will hold us accountable for what I did not say, and God will hold the people accountable for what they should have known had we been persuading them to the truth. The cultural milieu, no matter how steeped in the trenches of postmodern thought, cannot change the reality that God's Word is a plumb line by which all people will be measured. Be yourself, be authentic, but for the love of God, persuade.

The shepherd and the sheep follow the same Master. Since God's Word is so contrary to the common way of thinking, so different, so unique, it stands to reason that the preacher who explains Scripture must be persuasive. With all that is within him, he must gracefully and patiently call God's people to Himself.

THE PLACE OF PERSUASION

What bothers many is the sermon that uses persuasion to the exclusion of teaching and portraying. Certainly we have heard sermons where there was strong persuasion, but we were never quite sure what it was we were being persuaded to do. Persuasion is the handmaiden of teaching. It must always accompany teaching, and it must always follow teaching. Once the truth has been established, then persuasion should naturally flow as the logical expression of what to do with the revealed truth. In other words, a truth taught is simply an agreement between preacher and congregation. Persuasion calls the congregation to act on what has been taught. Augustine wrote,

> The eloquent divine, then, when he is urging a practical truth, must not only teach so as to give instruction, and please so as to keep up the attention, but he must also *sway the mind so as to subdue the will.*[7]

This seems very foreign. Why would a preacher want to "subdue the will"? Augustine continues:

> For if a man be not moved by the force of truth, though it is demonstrated to his own confession, and clothed in beauty

---

7. Augustine, *On Christian Doctrine*, trans. J. F. Shaw, Nicene and Post-Nicene Fathers, vol. 2, ed. Philip Schaff (Peabody: Hendrickson, 1994), XIII.29.

of style, nothing remains but to subdue him by the power of eloquence.[8]

What a powerful thought. Suppose you teach the truth clearly from a pure heart. As you teach, you paint the truth in such a way that people can see it clearly. In all integrity you represent the truth in plain fashion. Yet, there is no response. Augustine advocates that at this point, it is time to "sway the mind so as to subdue the will." Once the truth is clear, the preacher has the freedom and responsibility to press the truth home to the hearer in a way that is compelling, even forceful.

The will of the congregation is independent of that of the preacher. Each individual listening must yield his or her own consent to God. However, woe to us if we neglect, out of fear of excessive persuasion, to fully compel people to put themselves in obedience to Scripture.

CONCLUSION

Eloquence is teaching, portraying, and persuading. This simple approach is not Fénelon's alone. He borrowed heavily from Cicero and Augustine. In fact, this model is reflective of a broader classical approach to rhetoric. Why a classical model for postmodern times? The answer is simple.

During and before the time of Christ, the dominant religion was paganism. The center of paganism was false gods, and the result was hedonism, or complete self-indulgence. Christ's approach was simple: to teach about Himself and persuade people to follow Him. With the advent of the Enlightenment, the focus shifted to the mind above all else. This often is referred to as the beginning of modernity. In this present century, there is a rejection of the mind as ultimate and an embracing of the individual in his or her context. Truth is ultimately within the individual. Historically these are referred to as postmodern times. It is interesting that the result of postmodernism is the same as that of paganism, namely hedonism. In pagan times, Christ came

---

8. Ibid.

preaching Himself. Later followers, namely Augustine, would make full use of ancient models of rhetoric to call thousands to leave their hedonism and follow Christ. It was the ancient model; it was an effective model.

It is logical that the method that called people from hedonism in ancient paganism could call people from hedonism in the new paganism of postmodernity. While this is an oversimplification of history, it serves to show the plausibility of an ancient model for contemporary times. It was effective. It is effective.

[Conclusion]

Bearing the Cross in the Pulpit

The Difference Between Preaching and Yelling

And when the hour comes that he must speak, he ought,
before he opens his mouth, to lift up a thirsty soul to
God, to drink in what he is about to pour forth, and to
be himself filled with what he is about to distribute.

—Augustine

The year was 1935. On a large farm in Oklahoma, a young boy named Dalton Jennings felt the responsibility and freedom that came from farming life. He was up early, tended to his chores, and enjoyed a somewhat quiet early childhood. Yet, at the age of nine things changed.

A farming accident left his father with a head injury that caused severe hearing loss and occasional headaches. Like all in the farming community, Dalton's father simply got by in life and did the best he could with the limited help of rural medicine. He got along, that is, with one hitch: in order to communicate with him, Dalton and the entire family had to yell. And yell they did. In the morning and evening, the pleasant home was filled with continual yelling. There were

---

Epigraph. Augustine, *On Christian Doctrine*, trans. J. F. Shaw, Nicene and Post-Nicene Fathers, vol. 2, ed. Philip Schaff (Peabody: Hendrickson, 1994), 584.

no emotions involved, just loud voices bellowing in natural compensation for Dad's hearing loss.

When Dalton was fourteen, the local preacher was making conversation with his family after church and kindly said, "Son, maybe you will make a preacher one day."

"Oh, everyone preaches at our house, sir," Dalton quipped. It seems that preaching and yelling were the same for this quiet, precocious child. The pastor was so amused at this young man, he asked him to return that evening and read Scripture for "Christian Training Union" time.

Young Dalton unpretentiously approached the front of the church that afternoon, arousing only mild expectation from his listeners. He turned to Matthew 5 to read the Beatitudes and, knowing his dad was in the audience, proceeded to belt out the words of Christ in a thunderous voice. Neither the congregation nor Dalton had realized the vocal gift he had honed for years in the daily conversation of his home. The stunned crowd sat in silence at the quiet boy with the massive voice. When the pastor affirmed him after the service, Dalton simply replied, "I told you; everyone preaches at our house."

Dalton would soon win the hearts of his surprised family and friends in the small farming community. They loved him for his passion and his quiet demeanor that morphed into a thunderous voice when before a crowd.

Inevitably, Dalton would leave the farm to pursue training for Christian ministry. He returned a year later to preach both Sunday services at his home church. Dalton did not let on that he was disappointed with little success in his training and preaching. That afternoon he shared his frustration with his uneducated father, who had sensed something was wrong with the morning sermon. His father had always been silent on such matters, but a flood of bottled up wisdom poured out when he gave Dalton the secret that would change his life forever.

"Son, you can't preach because you have not listened. It's not that people don't listen to you; it's that you don't listen to God."

"But, Dad, I have the best voice of anyone my age!"

"Dalton, preaching is not people hearing you, preaching is people hearing God. I love you, son, but I'm afraid people can't hear God over your voice." Noticing the frustration in his son's eyes, he continued, "You preach too loud for people to hear God."

Dalton was bewildered at his father's presumption that he could tell him about ministry. Filled with anger at his dad's statements and fear that he might be right, he turned his back to his dad to walk away. How could the instrument that was used of God to open people's ears be the same instrument that kept them from hearing? Undaunted as Dalton walked away, the loving father continued in his loud, simple voice, "Son, don't you know how hard it is for me to hear?" His father continued to yell. "Every day I wake up, I strain to hear the smallest sound! But I don't care, because you learned your voice through my pain. I think I'm deaf so others won't have to be."

Dalton stopped with his back still to his dad.

"Now you have to go before God every day and strain to hear the voice of God. Listen hard to hear every little sound. And if you don't plan on hearing from God, my pain and your preaching will both be lost; so do us both a favor and farm. Or go in the house and don't come out till you've heard from God. My deafness gave you a voice; your deafness will take it away."

The truth of his father's words stung. They were the healing salt in his wounded ego. Dalton went to the house. Dalton begged for mercy. Dalton heard from God. When he entered the pulpit that night, he preached with the passion of a man who had heard from God. In that moment, Dalton realized that he stood on the shoulder of his father's pain every time he preached. And that if he did not strain to hear from the Father who saved him, he would waste the sacrifice and pain of the father who raised him.

Perhaps the greatest threat to the pulpit is the giftedness of its preachers. This work is offered for a generation that will surrender preaching so that every generation can hear God over our voices, a generation that will bear the cross in the pulpit in order to preach the cross from the pulpit, a generation dying to preach.